Teacher's Guide

H·E·A·R M·Y V·O·I·C·E

A multicultural anthology of literature from the United States

LAURIE KING

ADDISON-WESLEY PUBLISHING COMPANY

Menlo Park, California • Reading, Massachusetts • New York
Don Mills, Ontario • Wokingham, England • Amsterdam • Bonn
Paris • Milan • Madrid • Sydney • Singapore • Tokyo
Seoul • Taipei • Mexico City • San Juan

CONSULTANTS

Marie Duffey
Teacher
San Leandro High School
San Leandro, California

Jim Hopkins
Multicultural Consultant and Curriculum Developer
Cherokee Industries
Bellevue, Washington

This book is printed on recycled paper.

This book is published by Innovative Learning™, an imprint of Addison-Wesley's Alternative Publishing Group.

Project Editor: *Rachel Farber*
Production Manager: *Janet Yearian*
Production Coordinator: *Claire Flaherty*
Design Manager: *Jeff Kelly*
Design: *Seventeenth Street Studios*
Composition: *Publishing Support Services*

Cover Design: *Seventeenth Street Studios*
Cover art based on: Linda Lomahaftewa (Hopi/Choctaw), *New Mexico Sunset,* 1978. Acrylic on canvas, 130 X 104 cm. The Heard Museum, Pheonix. Photo courtesy of Linda Lomahaftewa.

ISBN 0-201-81840-X

3 4 5 6 7 8 - ML - 01 00 99 98

I was inspired by the thousands of teachers who adapt, create, experiment, love, and hang in there. In particular, I want to thank my family, friends, students, and colleagues who have taught me about cultures and about teaching. Thank you for bringing so much love and fun into your "lessons." You made this anthology and Teacher's Guide possible. To Manuela Apparicio Ryce, Gail Harter, Larry Emrich, Ginny Mickelson, Ginny Cotsis, Gabe Serrano and family, Gabino Aguirre and family, Luzma Espinoza and others in *Lucha*, Michael Mora, Linda Van der Wyck, Andy Sawyer, Jane Braunger, Linda Christiansen, Carlyn Syvanen, Maxine Rock and family, Carmen Meler and family, Gloria Johnson, Alice Goldfarb, Paul Artega and others at Chase Bag Company, Ted Cline, Ron Herndon and others in the Black United Front, my family on the East coast, and my students at Fillmore High School. Special thanks to Carol Mazer. Your suggestions have been right on. To the hundreds of political and social activists with whom I have worked—at kitchen tables and on picket lines—and to our goal of making this a multicultural, classless, nonsexist society.

To Robert Mangus, who was principal of Fillmore High School, thanks for boldly promoting heterogeneous grouping in English classes.

To Rachel Farber, my editor at Addison-Wesley, who is so intelligent, diplomatic, and fun to work with. I feel fortunate to have been able to work with you.

My special gratitude to Judith Wild, Jackie Ellenz, and my mother Sylvia Goldfarb, who all patiently listened to me through my writing process and gave me the precious gifts of their support, ideas, and care.

Dave King, my husband and partner for life . . . Your encouragement, inspiration, your ideas and outlook are in this project. You have been my partner in *Hear My Voice*.

To the memory of my father, Jack Goldfarb.

L.K.
Portland, Oregon

CONTENTS

Personal Identity

Celebrations

PREFACE

LIVING IN THE UNITED STATES PROVIDES teachers and students with experiences and observations about multiculturalism. Everyone has something to share and to learn on the subject. I hope this anthology and guide will give you, no matter where you live or were brought up, an opportunity to reinterpret, refine, and add to your experience of cultural diversity.

The United States is culturally diverse in many ways. Ethnicity, socioeconomic status, religious beliefs, gender, and sexual orientation are part of culture. Physical and mental abilities are factors in culture. In addition, individual families often have their own cultures. The literature in the anthology and the lessons in this guide primarily explore culture as it relates to ethnicity, family, and class, but are relevant to all dimensions of diversity.

I grew up in New York in the 1950s and 1960s, and, like countless Jewish kids, I felt Chanukah and Passover could not hold a candle to Christmas and Easter. Even in New York City, when I was a child, Chanukah was barely mentioned in the media and school. In school, we made Christmas cards, ate Christmas cookies, and brought in Christmas presents for a party. Being so trained in what was worthy, what did I want at home? A Christmas tree, tinsel, cards; I wanted to be American. My parents' eyes hardened. "No! Don't even ask," was the answer. I felt I was being denied something essential, that I was being kept apart and "different." Had my school included Chanukah and Passover in its seasonal celebrations, I might have had a more positive response to my own culture.

Even today, by often omitting the accomplishments and point of view of people of diverse cultures, we have the power to "teach" young people that their community and ancestors have little to offer. Such omissions have affected people of different cultures to varying degrees. Native American, African American, Latino, Asian American, and some European American cultures exist very tenuously in the school curriculum today. Fortunately, we also have the power to introduce students to the significant contributions and importance of people of all cultures. A fundamental goal of multicultural education, including the study of multicultural literature, is to bring to light voices and points of view that have previously been hidden from public view.

Are students conscious of the relative omission of some cultures from the school curriculum? At a high school in Southern California a group of us in the faculty invited predominantly Chicano and Mexican students to an inservice to describe what it was like to attend the school. The outpouring of feelings made a lasting impression on me and on most other faculty members.

In answering questions and telling stories, what emerged was that even though Mexican Americans were by far in the majority in the town and school, these students felt they did not belong. They felt invisible. That word was used again and again. Such perceived invisibility was a response to the underrepresentation of their culture, language, history, traditions, and stories in the curriculum. Each student felt that he or she as a real person was not seen.

Closely related to the feeling of invisibility were feelings of not belonging. One of the top students in the school, a junior from a Mexican family, said, to the audience's amazement, that she could not walk into the administration building if the Chicano vice-principal were not present. This, she said, was because she felt so intimidated. "I do not belong here. I do not feel that it is my school." This was a young woman so gifted she could eloquently analyze Shakespeare and Twain even though her family spoke no English at home. She traveled the route of many working class Chicanas: she became a young mother, choosing to stay close to her family and community and giving up a scholarship to Stanford.

Perhaps she was feeling what a young man, a brilliant senior, felt when he said that school was "too different from home." He could not hold it together and he thought he would probably return to Mexico as did his brother. There was such a stark division between family and community, on the one hand, and the culture of the school on the other, that many students felt they had to make a painful choice. They felt they could not achieve a balance.

What happens when we begin to incorporate students' cultures into the classroom? How does it make students feel? What kinds of responses do they have? You may have answers to these questions from your own experiences. Try the lessons in this book, and make up your own lessons. Crafting a multicultural curriculum is entering relatively uncharted and infinitely exciting territory.

An example of the power of working within students' cultures is shown in a lesson that I discovered in my English class in Southern California, and it is included in the lesson plans. The first bilingual poem I read was "This Is the Land" by Carlos Cortez, and I found it especially evocative. The Spanish words, even when I needed to use the footnotes for translations, added to the meaning of the poem. I suddenly thought, why not have students write their own bilingual poems? Such an activity would validate the skills of those who are bilingual and give them the chance to reaffirm their expertise by teaching others.

Using Carl Sandberg's poem "Chicago" as a model, students wrote poems about a place. I asked them to choose a setting in which at least two languages are spoken and to include at least three non-English words in their poems. Since most wrote about a place in which Spanish and English are spoken, those who were not fluent in Spanish consulted those who were. As a class we had fun filling the three large blackboards surrounding the classroom with translations: *naranja*—orange; *flor*—blossom; *fragrancia*—fragrance; *ruido*—noise; *aburrido*—boring.

The bilingual poetry validated the language of the Chicano students' lives because the Spanish words enhanced the meaning and feelings expressed by these poems. The hidden meaning of this lesson was that these students' communities, their parents, and thus they themselves, offer something beautiful, unique, and valuable. The lesson also taught these young people that the school had high expectations of more quality work from them.

Furthermore, learning collectively and using Spanish expressions gave the European-American students the chance, too rare in our society, to validate another culture. It gave them the chance to learn from others, to work collaboratively, and to achieve deeper meaning in their poems.

The following are two such poems, the first by a Mexican-American student, the second by a European-American student. Neither young man would characterize himself as being at ease with poetry.

FILLMORE/FILTROS[1]

Fillmore is just a town
with not much to do.
Half Hispanic and half Anglo.
No one cares who is best,
or who is worst.
Las fiestas[2] are the only things that come alive.
Las calles[3] seem deserted at night
with the wind blowing the leaves
from place to place.
A few people gather, but
not much to do.
It's just another day
in el pueblo[4] de Fillmore.   —*Eric Rangel*

BROTHERS AND SISTERS

Brothers and sisters, you may ask,
Who are our brothers and sisters?
In this place we call them friends.
Who is our friend?
Is it the local grocery store owner?
Or maybe the paper boy?
Or maybe it's only our own color we speak with.
We call it prejudice in this place.
I call it stupidity!
Who needs it?

What happened to the little kid in us?
Has it grown up
so that we can't celebrate un compleano de un amigo?[5]
Why must we fight and call each other names?

---

1. Fillmore's nickname in Spanish is "Filtros."
2. Las fiestas—the parties
3. Los calles—the streets
4. el pueblo—the town
5. Un compleano de un amigo—a friend's birthday

"Hey wetback!" "Hey gringo," we hear everyday.
Have our hearts grown too calloused?
Is it too late for us?
Can't we just be amigable y simpatico?[1]
Or must we be antipatico,[2] menso?[3]
Let's put away our foolishness,
and just accept each other for who we are.
Are you listening?
Let's just be hermanos y hermanas.[4]   —*Ben Wall*

I have found that because a pluralist curriculum is relatively new, I have sometimes had to introduce lessons with extra patience. Many students will not be accustomed to the material. For example, many students have learned from bitter experience to be suspicious when people of cultures other than their own bring up their heritage. Some of my African-American eighth-grade students in Portland, Oregon, begged me to allow them to leave the room or turn their seats around when I showed the class movies about African cultures. When I asked them why, they said that they "knew the movie would be stupid." One student said that it would probably be about jungles. Students' responses are valid, and a patient attitude is essential in developing trust.

A point often overlooked in discussions of multicultural education is that a curriculum including the study of diverse cultures will enhance the writing and thinking of people from the United States' most assimilated cultures as well as those whose cultures are omitted from public view. Multicultural literature pays profound attention to roots and traditions. Respect for roots is significant for the many Americans whose traditions and cultures have been boiled beyond recognition in the melting pot. Studying multicultural literature will likely help people of all cultures recognize the power of and revitalize their ethnic, community, and family traditions.

We live in perhaps the most multicultural society the world has ever known. Everyone has positive and negative experiences related to this diversity. Let us each, in our classrooms, help nurture, refine, and appre-

---

1. amigable y simpatico—friendly and intimate, sensitive
2. antipatico—mean
3. menso—silly
4. hermanos y hermanas—brothers and sisters

ciate our own and each other's cultures. The best curriculum development comes with our own ideas and our own work. I hope the projects in this guide will be enjoyable and provocative for educators as well as students.

USING *HEAR MY VOICE* IN YOUR CLASSROOM

A THEMATIC ORGANIZATION ALLOWS YOU TO INFUSE LITERATURE FROM A VARIETY OF CULTURES INTO YOUR CURRENT COURSE OF STUDY.

The thematic organization of *Hear My Voice* is designed to allow you to easily infuse selections from the anthology as well as selected longer works into your existing curriculum. In my years of teaching literature to high school students, I've come to realize that students have the most success comparing, and consequently understanding, works of literature about similar topics. Thus, I've organized the anthology and lessons in the Teacher's Guide into six thematic units: Borders; Love; Family and Generations; Society: Conflict, Struggle, and Change; Personal Identity; and Celebrations. I suggest studying the anthology works in each of these units along with corresponding works you already use in your classroom. For instance, if your class already reads *King Lear*, you may wish to choose anthology selections from the Family and Generations unit.

For all lessons about literature, I have provided a list of anthology selections and longer works which I feel fit the lesson. In some cases you may wish to suggest particular works to students, and in others you may wish to ask students to choose works that they think are appropriate to the lesson. The selected longer works reflect a variety of cultures and include some books currently standard in many high school and college English courses across the United States. The *Hear My Voice Bibliography* contains annotated reviews of two hundred fiction and nonfiction works reflecting the themes of the anthology and Teacher's Guide. Selected longer works included in the *Hear My Voice Bibliography* are denoted with an asterisk (*). In addition to my suggestions, you will likely develop many other ways to weave together the different strands of literature from the United States.

If literature by and about people from a variety of cultures and ethnic groups is not infused into a course of study, but is instead represented in special weeks or in brief sections of a course, students will receive the impression that certain cultures have only a peripheral status in our society. James Banks, author of *Multicultural Education: Issues and Perspectives* (Boston: Allyn & Bacon), outlines the four levels of integration of multicultural materials: the contributions approach which introduces people, holidays, and other discrete elements; the additive approach whereby multicultural themes and perspectives are added to the curriculum without changing the core structure; the transformational approach in which the curriculum structure is changed to enable students to view issues, events, and themes from a variety of perspectives; and the social action approach which teaches students to think critically, make decisions on social issues, and take actions to help solve them. I hope the *Hear My Voice* program enables you to fully engage students on the highest level, the social action approach.

R. Richard Banks, former director of Stanford University's Upward Bound program, underlines the value of infusing the study of all cultures into a curriculum when he says, "I look forward to the day when Black History Month is abolished. While many have learned from the events that fill each February, Black History Month's continuance signals that the hope from which it sprang remains unrealized."

HOW TO WEAVE *HEAR MY VOICE* INTO YOUR PROGRAM: FOUR OPTIONS

OPTION 1:
Use Hear My Voice *as the primary text in a full-year American literature program in high school or college.*

If you use this option, I recommend that you use one-half to two-thirds of the selections in each section of the anthology. You will probably also wish to study longer works of fiction and nonfiction. Assign supplementary longer materials from your existing curriculum or from the *Hear My Voice Bibliography*. Use lessons in the Teacher's Guide to help you teach the literature in the anthology as well as the selected longer works.

OPTION 2:
Use Hear My Voice *as the primary text in a half-year American literature course in high school or college.*

Intersperse one-third to one-half of the selections in each section of the anthology with other works you usually study. As in Option 1, assign longer works from your existing curriculum or from the *Hear My Voice Bibliography*. Use the Teacher's Guide to help you teach the literature in the anthology as well as some of the selected longer works.

OPTION 3:
Use Hear My Voice *as a companion to other works studied in grades nine through twelve English and social studies classes and in college classes.*

If you choose this option, you may wish to collaborate with teachers within your department to decide which material from *Hear My Voice* to use at each grade level. For example, you may decide to incorporate several selections from the section Love into a study of *Romeo and Juliet*. Likewise, some of the selections in Personal Identity would complement *The Catcher in the Rye*, which is commonly studied in the tenth grade. Other selections in Personal Identity are easily related to *Hamlet*. Many lessons in the Teacher's Guide facilitate this infusion. You may also wish to present longer works of literature from a variety of cultures throughout the four years.

OPTION 4:
Combine uses of Hear My Voice.

With this option, teachers coordinate their programs so that *Hear My Voice* is used as a full-year text in the eleventh grade and as a companion book in the other grades. The bulk of the selections are reserved for the eleventh grade, but appropriate works are taught throughout the high school years. The Teacher's Guide lessons can be used for grades nine through twelve.

All of the above options can substantially enrich a high school or college's literature program. I believe multicultural literature should be infused into any American literature course, so I suggest you use the *Hear My Voice Bibliography* to find works appropriate for your classroom.

FOCUS ON OPEN-ENDED CRITICAL THINKING

I have attempted to construct lessons that serve as frameworks within which students can discover truths about literature, their personal lives, and political and social realities. To explore the cultural diversity of the

United States is to enter relatively new territory, thus the focus on discovery is particularly appropriate. Questions in the anthology and Teacher's Guide seldom call for a correct answer, but instead encourage divergent thinking. Adequate responses require reflection, research, writing, and interaction. I will discuss assessment of such work later in this chapter.

CONTROVERSIAL ISSUES

I have found that the exploration of cultures engages students and touches their lives in ways that may be unusual in language arts or social studies classes. Due to the intensity of such study and the nature of the material, you need to be prepared for controversial issues to emerge.

What are some likely areas of controversy? Students and educators may disagree about how much attention should be given to study of cultural diversity. Readers will also have differences of opinion regarding which characterizations in literary works are stereotypical and which expressions are offensive. Further, students will likely discuss a variety of solutions to problems of discrimination, prejudice, and racism. An open, accepting, and safe classroom atmosphere in which critical thinking is encouraged allows each student to develop his or her own views about the literary selections and the issues that emerge.

I have attempted to avoid including in the anthology selections that contain stereotypes. A small number of the suggested longer works may contain characterizations or expressions that can be interpreted as stereotypical. Should any member of the class feel that a certain culture is portrayed in a stereotypical manner in a literary work, you may wish to take the opportunity to conduct a class discussion on the topic. Stereotyping is treated directly in lessons in Borders and in Society: Conflict, Struggle, and Change.

Two areas of controversy are of particular concern to educators: the use of sexual language and cursing in the literary selections. I have attempted to keep such language to a minimum within the anthology, but this was not possible with all the suggested longer works. If you are unfamiliar with the longer works listed in the Teacher's Guide lessons, I suggest that you refer to the *Hear My Voice Bibliography* (ISBN 0-201-81841-8) in which these books are reviewed. In the bibliography I have noted whether the books contain occasional or frequent sexual references or strong language.

My personal view is that students can gain insight and maturity through the study of quality literature that deals with sexuality when the school community is supportive. Structured and open discussions of these issues in the classroom can help students make reasoned decisions and judgments outside of the classroom.

ASSESSING STUDENTS' UNDERSTANDING AND ACHIEVEMENT

How can we assess students' understanding and achievement as they read the literature and engage in the activities outlined in *Hear My Voice?* First I will examine some general issues related to assessment in the language arts, and then I will discuss issues that pertain more specifically to *Hear My Voice*.

I believe frequent assessment of students' understanding and achievement should occur and that such assessment provide opportunities for learning. As much as possible, assessment should help members of the class gain understanding of the course materials. For instance, a brief oral quiz assessing comprehension of a short story or part of a novel can be used to identify students who have missed or misunderstood a crucial episode and to help them return to the work with a clearer understanding of the material. Instead of falling further behind, these students can approach the next assignment with more confidence.

The more a variety of assignments and assessments are related to each other, the greater student achievement will be. Overlaying different kinds of assignments about the same material deepens understanding of the text or topic. I suggest that you choose a number of the following assignments as you study a topic or work of literature: individual, pair, and group journal writing; oral quizzes; visual interpretations of literature; speeches; discussions and debates; skits; writing fiction and essays; viewing and critiquing relevant films.

A number of the lessons in this guide involve essay or fiction writing. You may wish to plan a series of smaller assignments leading up to major essays, tests, or fiction writing. Such a sequence, especially if some parts of it are carefully assessed, increases the likelihood of student success in the larger assignments.

You may find careful evaluation of each assignment unnecessary or impractical. In many cases, you may wish to simply record that students have completed the assignment. In other cases, you can evaluate assignments as part of oral classwork or visual displays. Also, students can learn to review the work of their classmates. Such peer editing sharpens students' critical skills and often makes students more receptive to constructive criticism about their own work. I like to employ a combination of these tactics, taking care that I carefully read and write comments on a number of the smaller assignments, especially when they are crucial for the successful completion of a major assignment.

I also require that students keep literary journals and portfolios of their work. I allow my students some sessions of journal writing that they can keep totally private, and at other times, which are announced in advance, the topic is one which they may be expected to share with the class.

Evaluation and grading require serious consideration. What criteria should teachers use? This question assumes particular importance when curriculum is primarily based on reading and responding to literature. Many of the questions in *Hear My Voice* and lessons in the Teacher's Guide encourage divergent thinking; they do not lead to a single correct answer. How then can we evaluate and grade student understanding?

I approach this issue directly with my students. One of my primary objectives is to help my students learn to recognize and understand the difference between factual questions and interpretive questions about a work of literature. Although such a line is not always easy to draw, critical thinkers can usually distinguish between issues of fact and issues of thought or interpretation. All students are responsible for having correct answers on questions of fact, and all students are expected to explore and interpret literature and to justify or support their views.

I must frequently remind myself that it is far more important for students to interpret and support their own views than to learn my view of a work of literature, no matter how edifying and justifiable I consider my view. If we teachers constantly judge students' responses, students will shy away from expressing original thoughts and responses. In an open classroom atmosphere in which everyone, including the teacher, expresses opinions and relevant justification, members of the class have an opportunity to revise their opinions in a reasonable manner.

When grading, I look for the amount of effort and time students have invested into their projects. Improvement is the key to my grading. In the course of a semester and within assignments that require stages of revision, I expect students to improve their thinking skills, to take greater risks in expressing their opinions or interpretations, and to become more sophisticated in supporting their views.

In major writing assignments, I grade the first draft on generation of ideas. I expect the last draft to show revision and improvement in the following areas: depth of detail, organization, grammar, mechanics, and presentation. In order to help students revise their work, I teach lessons throughout the semester on grammar, usage, and style. These small lessons often provide opportunities for other types of evaluation.

CONNECTING WITH THE COMMUNITY

Studying literature by authors of diverse cultures provides an excellent opportunity to engage members of the community who might not often participate in school activities. As appropriate, lessons in the Teacher's Guide encourage teachers to invite parents and other community members to serve as linguistic and cultural resources. Some lessons also encourage inviting community members into the school for displays of student work, readings, and celebrations.

MAKING CROSS-CURRICULAR CONNECTIONS

Multicultural literature and social studies are natural friends: the study of one illuminates the other. I have included social studies questions in the anthology and social studies lessons in the Teacher's Guide. At the end of this chapter, I have included two model social studies lessons that may be applied to many works of literature. Following the social studies model lessons is a chart that correlates anthology selections to United States history topics as found in Addison-Wesley's *The United States and Its People.* This handy reference will enable you to connect literary selections with relevant social studies concepts as appropriate for your classroom.

Because many students enjoy art and because of the natural connection between literature and the visual arts, I have also included a variety of lessons that call for a visual response to literature.

WRITING AS A RESPONSE TO LITERATURE

Many lessons in the Teacher's Guide involve writing. Literature by authors of diverse cultures and backgrounds provides excellent ideas and models for student writers. The writing activities in this book are also intended to help students reach their own conclusions about the literature they read.

I have not presented a specific version of a writing process as part of the lessons, but, like many other teachers, I encourage students to approach major writing projects with a process that includes prewriting, drafting, response, and editing procedures. I have included extensive prewriting prompts for most lessons involving writing.

I feel that having an authentic audience is one of the greatest motivators of student writing. If students write for an assignment thinking that the teacher will be the sole reader, then their writing will be much different than if they were writing with a classmate, family member, or neighbor in mind. To this end, I recommend that you create opportunities for students to share their work and help students publish their writing for distribution in their own communities.

INDIVIDUAL LEARNING VS. COLLABORATIVE LEARNING

In general, I have not specified whether students should work individually, in pairs, in cooperative groups, or as a class. This seems to be an area that is best left to the individual teacher. If your students work in groups, you may want to have groups of students read different novels, plays, or shorter works, and use the same lessons for the different works.

ORGANIZATION OF LESSONS IN THE TEACHER'S GUIDE

The lessons in the Teacher's Guide are grouped by units corresponding to the anthology and are of three types: those that relate to one selection in the anthology; those that relate to a number of selections in the anthology, as well as selected longer works; and those which do not relate directly to any particular work in the anthology, but serve as general introductions or conclusions to many works of literature. Although I have provided many specific suggestions, you will probably identify lessons that work well with some of your own favorite pieces of literature.

The general text is addressed to the teacher. Prewriting prompts, discussion questions, and direct student instruction are in italics and are addressed to students.

THE SOCIAL STUDIES CONNECTION:
TWO MODEL LESSONS

WHETHER YOU TEACH language arts, social studies, or a course that integrates both subjects, exploring and discovering the connections between the two subjects makes them both more powerful for students.

MODEL LESSON I

The purpose of this lesson is to help students gain historical background on a work of literature before they begin to read the work. This early familiarity will enhance students' understanding as they read the literature.

1. Provide students with a list of significant places, events, trends, and concepts to research. For instance, students about to embark on reading Ralph Ellison's *Invisible Man* might research Harlem in the 1930s and 1940s. If your class is preparing to read Leslie Marmon Silko's *Storyteller*, you may wish to have students research the geography of New Mexico.

2. Students may present their research in a variety of formats:

   • factual reports

   • I-Search papers (see page 93 for a detailed lesson on I-Search papers)

   • fictionalized letters or diary entries based on the information they discover

Fictionalized letters and diaries are an effective way to present information. After students research Harlem in the 1930s and 1940s, for instance, you might assign them to write a letter home in the voice of a young man or woman who migrated to Harlem from a town in the rural south in 1940. The young man or woman would send impressions of Harlem home to family, friends, or a sweetheart.

This social studies lesson is intended to be used while students are reading a particular work or after the class has completed reading that work. First, students generate questions to help focus their research on historical and geographical aspects of the literature, and then they write I-Search reports on a topic of their choice. This lesson differs from Model Lesson I because in this case the students generate their questions about the literature.

Let us look at a specific example. Assume that your class is reading Frank Chin's *Donald Duk*, a novel about a twelve-year-old Chinese-American boy who begins to learn about Chinese-American history, especially Chinese-American labor history. You may decide to enhance understanding of this fastpaced and humorous book set in contemporary San Francisco's Chinatown by having your class inquire into the historical and cultural background of the novel.

I. Work with the class to generate topics and questions that are based on students' real questions about the book. The results of a brainstorming session for *Donald Duk* might look something like this:

a. *What is the history of San Francisco's Chinatown?*
   - *When was it settled?*
   - *How has it changed over the years?*
   - *Has the size and nature of the population changed? How?*
   - *What do the buildings look like?*
   - *Do non-Chinese people live there?*
   - *Are there Chinatown public schools?*
   - *What kinds of churches are in Chinatown?*
   - *What were "tongs"? Do they still exist?*
   - *Are there really gangs in Chinatown? If so, what are they like?*

b. *What is the history of Chinese laborers in the United States, especially on the railroads?*
   - *How many Chinese railroad workers were in the United States?*
   - *When did the workers come?*
   - *What were they told about conditions in the United States?*
   - *What were the conditions for the laborers in regard to food, housing, family life, wages, health, and religion?*
   - *What was the process of building the railroad?*

- *Were Chinese laborers in unions?*
- *Where did the workers go when the railroads were completed?*
- *Is Chin's account of the "Golden Spike" ceremony accurate?*

Participating in such a brainstorming session should give all students enough ideas to begin research. Once they begin their I-Search journals, some students are likely to find related topics that they wish to pursue further for their reports. Other students will want to choose one of the original topics. Students should use encyclopedias, specialized history books, biographies, and geography books for their research.

Integrating Literature and Social Studies: Borders

Selections from *Hear My Voice*

Chapter Number, Title, and Time Period*	Seventh Grade	In Response to Executive Order ...	Who Said We All Have to Talk Alike	Paths Upon Water	Notes from a Fragmented Daughter	Different Cultural Levels Eat Here	I'll Crack Your Head Kotsun	"Mommy, What Does 'Nigger' Mean?"	A Seat in the Garden	We Wear the Mask	Sonrisas	A Song in the Front Yard	Doors	Nikki-Rosa
1. An Unfinished Story	•		•	•	•			•					•	
2. Bridges to a New Land 20,000 B.C.–A.D. 1700														
3. Creating a New Society 1600–1763									•					
4. The Struggle for Independence 1763–1783														
5. Beginnings of a Nation 1776–1787														
6. Creating the Constitution 1787–1791														
7. Setting Democracy in Motion 1789–1801														
8. The Growth of the Nation 1801–1828														
9. Conflict and Reform 1828–1850														
10. The West: Crossroads of Cultures 1820–1850														
11. The Gathering Storm 1850–1861														
12. The Civil War 1861–1865														
13. The Struggle Over the South's Future 1865–1905														
14. Forces Shaping a New West 1850–1910														
15. The Age of Industry 1865–1910														
16. Politics and Poverty in the Gilded Age 1865–1910														
17. The Impulse for Social Justice 1900–1917										•				
18. Reaching for World Power 1890–1916						•								
19. The First World War 1914–1920														
20. The Twenties: Blowing the Lid Off 1919–1928						•								
21. From Boom to Bust 1928–1932														
22. The New Deal 1932–1939														
23. A Fragile Peace 1920–1941														
24. The Second World War 1941–1945		•		•				•						
25. A Beacon to the World 1945–1960														
26. Abundance and Uncertainty 1945–1960				•				•						
27. Camelot and the Great Society 1960–1968												•		•
28. "Let Justice Roll Down" 1954–1968	•							•						•
29. The Ordeal of Vietnam 1954–1975														
30. The Unsettled Seventies 1969–1980	•							•	•		•		•	
31. New Directions 1980–Present												•		•
32. The United States in a Changing World	•		•	•	•			•	•		•		•	

The United States and Its People, Addison-Wesley Publishing Company, 1993

Integrating Literature and Social Studies: Love

Chapter Number, Title, and Time Period*	Selections from *Hear My Voice*									
	Family Dinner	Juke Box Love Song	From *Children of the River*	She is Beautiful in Her Whole Being	A Certain Beginning	Anniversary	Finding a Wife	Never Offer Your Heart …	The Pieces/Fragmentos	When Your Eyes Speak/Cuando …
1. An Unfinished Story	●		●							
2. Bridges to a New Land 20,000 B.C.–A.D. 1700				●						
3. Creating a New Society 1600–1763										
4. The Struggle for Independence 1763–1783										
5. Beginnings of a Nation 1776–1787										
6. Creating the Constitution 1787–1791										
7. Setting Democracy in Motion 1789–1801										
8. The Growth of the Nation 1801–1828										
9. Conflict and Reform 1828–1850										
10. The West: Crossroads of Cultures 1820–1850										
11. The Gathering Storm 1850–1861										
12. The Civil War 1861–1865										
13. The Struggle Over the South's Future 1865–1905										
14. Forces Shaping a New West 1850–1910										
15. The Age of Industry 1865–1910										
16. Politics and Poverty in the Gilded Age 1865–1910										
17. The Impulse for Social Justice 1900–1917										
18. Reaching for World Power 1890–1916										
19. The First World War 1914–1920										
20. The Twenties: Blowing the Lid Off 1919–1928		●								
21. From Boom to Bust 1928–1932										
22. The New Deal 1932–1939										
23. A Fragile Peace 1920–1941										
24. The Second World War 1941–1945										
25. A Beacon to the World 1945–1960										
26. Abundance and Uncertainty 1945–1960	●									
27. Camelot and the Great Society 1960–1968						●				
28. "Let Justice Roll Down" 1954–1968										
29. The Ordeal of Vietnam 1954–1975			●			●				
30. The Unsettled Seventies 1969–1980					●			●	●	●
31. New Directions 1980–Present					●			●		
32. The United States in a Changing World	●			●	●					

*The United States and Its People, Addison-Wesley Publishing Company, 1993

Integrating Literature and Social Studies: Family and Generations

Chapter Number, Title, and Time Period*	Selections from *Hear My Voice*	In Search of Our Mothers' Gardens	A Moving Day	Ancestor	Those Winter Sundays	The Morning My Father Died…	The Bending of a Twig	Scribbles	I Stand Here Ironing	Indian Boarding School…	The Poet Imagines His…	From *A Bintel Brief: Letters*…	In the American Society	Poem Near Midway Truck Stop	My Mother's Stories	Girl
1. An Unfinished Story	●															
2. Bridges to a New Land 20,000 B.C.–A.D. 1700																
3. Creating a New Society 1600–1763	●															
4. The Struggle for Independence 1763–1783																
5. Beginnings of a Nation 1776–1787	●															
6. Creating the Constitution 1787–1791																
7. Setting Democracy in Motion 1789–1801																
8. The Growth of the Nation 1801–1828																
9. Conflict and Reform 1828–1850	●															
10. The West: Crossroads of Cultures 1820–1850																
11. The Gathering Storm 1850–1861	●															
12. The Civil War 1861–1865	●															
13. The Struggle Over the South's Future 1865–1905	●															
14. Forces Shaping a New West 1850–1910									●							
15. The Age of Industry 1865–1910										●	●			●		
16. Politics and Poverty in the Gilded Age 1865–1910																
17. The Impulse for Social Justice 1900–1917																
18. Reaching for World Power 1890–1916																
19. The First World War 1914–1920																
20. The Twenties: Blowing the Lid Off 1919–1928	●															
21. From Boom to Bust 1928–1932	●							●								
22. The New Deal 1932–1939								●						●		
23. A Fragile Peace 1920–1941			●													
24. The Second World War 1941–1945			●													
25. A Beacon to the World 1945–1960																
26. Abundance and Uncertainty 1945–1960																
27. Camelot and the Great Society 1960–1968																
28. "Let Justice Roll Down" 1954–1968																
29. The Ordeal of Vietnam 1954–1975																
30. The Unsettled Seventies 1969–1980			●				●		●							
31. New Directions 1980–Present																
32. The United States in a Changing World			●	●								●				

The United States and Its People, Addison-Wesley Publishing Company, 1993

Integrating Literature and Social Studies: Society: Conflict, Struggle, and Change

Chapter Number, Title, and Time Period*	Selections from *Hear My Voice*	Wasichus in the Hills	Concentration Constellation	The Lesson	Letter from a Birmingham Jail	I Have a Dream	Poems from *Songs of Gold Mountain*	Each Year Grain	They Say Them Child Brides ...	Tony's Story	This Is the Land
1. An Unfinished Story				●	●	●					●
2. Bridges to a New Land 20,000 B.C.–A.D. 1700											●
3. Creating a New Society 1600–1763											
4. The Struggle for Independence 1763–1783											
5. Beginnings of a Nation 1776–1787											
6. Creating the Constitution 1787–1791											
7. Setting Democracy in Motion 1789–1801											
8. The Growth of the Nation 1801–1828											
9. Conflict and Reform 1828–1850		●									
10. The West: Crossroads of Cultures 1820–1850		●									
11. The Gathering Storm 1850–1861											
12. The Civil War 1861–1865											
13. The Struggle Over the South's Future 1865–1905											
14. Forces Shaping a New West 1850–1910		●						●			●
15. The Age of Industry 1865–1910							●	●			
16. Politics and Poverty in the Gilded Age 1865–1910								●	●		
17. The Impulse for Social Justice 1900–1917									●		
18. Reaching for World Power 1890–1916											
19. The First World War 1914–1920											
20. The Twenties: Blowing the Lid Off 1919–1928									●		
21. From Boom to Bust 1928–1932									●		
22. The New Deal 1932–1939											
23. A Fragile Peace 1920–1941											
24. The Second World War 1941–1945			●								
25. A Beacon to the World 1945–1960											
26. Abundance and Uncertainty 1945–1960											
27. Camelot and the Great Society 1960–1968											
28. "Let Justice Roll Down" 1954–1968				●	●	●					
29. The Ordeal of Vietnam 1954–1975											
30. The Unsettled Seventies 1969–1980				●				●		●	●
31. New Directions 1980–Present				●							
32. The United States in a Changing World											

The United States and Its People, Addison-Wesley Publishing Company, 1993

Integrating Literature and Social Studies: Personal Identity

Chapter Number, Title, and Time Period*	Selections from *Hear My Voice*	My Dungeon Shook...	Ending Poem	Freeway 280	From *I Know Why the Caged Bird Sings*	From *Donald Duk*	Flying Home	Autumn Gardening	South Brooklyn, 1947	Ellis Island	Going Home	Choices
1. An Unfinished Story	●											
2. Bridges to a New Land 20,000 B.C.–A.D. 1700										●	●	
3. Creating a New Society 1600–1763										●	●	
4. The Struggle for Independence 1763–1783												
5. Beginnings of a Nation 1776–1787											●	
6. Creating the Constitution 1787–1791												
7. Setting Democracy in Motion 1789–1801												
8. The Growth of the Nation 1801–1828												
9. Conflict and Reform 1828–1850												
10. The West: Crossroads of Cultures 1820–1850												
11. The Gathering Storm 1850–1861												
12. The Civil War 1861–1865	●											
13. The Struggle Over the South's Future 1865–1905												
14. Forces Shaping a New West 1850–1910										●		
15. The Age of Industry 1865–1910									●	●		
16. Politics and Poverty in the Gilded Age 1865–1910												
17. The Impulse for Social Justice 1900–1917												
18. Reaching for World Power 1890–1916												
19. The First World War 1914–1920												
20. The Twenties: Blowing the Lid Off 1919–1928				●					●			
21. From Boom to Bust 1928–1932												
22. The New Deal 1932–1939				●								
23. A Fragile Peace 1920–1941												
24. The Second World War 1941–1945						●	●					
25. A Beacon to the World 1945–1960												
26. Abundance and Uncertainty 1945–1960				●					●			
27. Camelot and the Great Society 1960–1968												
28. "Let Justice Roll Down" 1954–1968	●											
29. The Ordeal of Vietnam 1954–1975												
30. The Unsettled Seventies 1969–1980		●	●								●	●
31. New Directions 1980–Present	●					●						
32. The United States in a Changing World	●	●	●			●						●

The United States and Its People, Addison-Wesley Publishing Company, 1993

Integrating Literature and Social Studies: Celebrations

Chapter Number, Title, and Time Period*	Selections from *Hear My Voice*														
	Chumash Man	Ain't That Bad?	Call Letters: Mrs. V. B.	Theresa's Friends	Flipochinos	Powwow 79, Durango	Deer Woman	In the Beginning	The Latest Latin Dance Craze	Carlos De Oxnard	The Woman Who Makes Swell…	Ravioli	Rice Planting	To Satch: American Gothic	The English Lesson
1. An Unfinished Story			●		●					●		●	●		●
2. Bridges to a New Land 20,000 B.C.–A.D. 1700	●			●	●					●					
3. Creating a New Society 1600–1763															
4. The Struggle for Independence 1763–1783															
5. Beginnings of a Nation 1776–1787															
6. Creating the Constitution 1787–1791															
7. Setting Democracy in Motion 1789–1801															
8. The Growth of the Nation 1801–1828															
9. Conflict and Reform 1828–1850															
10. The West: Crossroads of Cultures 1820–1850						●									
11. The Gathering Storm 1850–1861				●											
12. The Civil War 1861–1865															
13. The Struggle Over the South's Future 1865–1905															
14. Forces Shaping a New West 1850–1910						●									
15. The Age of Industry 1865–1910				●						●	●	●			
16. Politics and Poverty in the Gilded Age 1865–1910															
17. The Impulse for Social Justice 1900–1917														●	
18. Reaching for World Power 1890–1916					●										
19. The First World War 1914–1920															
20. The Twenties: Blowing the Lid Off 1919–1928										●				●	
21. From Boom to Bust 1928–1932															
22. The New Deal 1932–1939										●					
23. A Fragile Peace 1920–1941															
24. The Second World War 1941–1945				●						●			●		
25. A Beacon to the World 1945–1960															
26. Abundance and Uncertainty 1945–1960														●	
27. Camelot and the Great Society 1960–1968															
28. "Let Justice Roll Down" 1954–1968															
29. The Ordeal of Vietnam 1954–1975															
30. The Unsettled Seventies 1969–1980						●				●					●
31. New Directions 1980–Present															
32. The United States in a Changing World		●				●				●		●	●		●

*The United States and Its People, Addison-Wesley Publishing Company, 1993

BORDERS

*B*ORDERS EXIST IN MANY FORMS. The Rio Grande defines a border between countries. 96th Street in New York City defines a border between downtown and Harlem. Countries have borders between them, and our multicultural society has borders within it. Some of these borders within the United States are lines between communities and neighborhoods; others may be found where people of different cultures meet—even in one room. Borders may be lively, exhilarating, colorful places, or they may be tense, even violent places. Cultures interplay in a variety of ways: they can clash, one can dominate the other, they can mock each other, stare at each other, ignore each other, blend to different degrees, and combine to produce new, sometimes fantastic, forms.

At this point in our history, borders have a mixed record. There are borders at which a dominant group attempts to keep others "in their place." Other borders, however, define zones that are enjoyable or comfortable places to be for members of a given culture. Individuals or groups have differing points of view about the desirability and fairness of certain borders. This area of controversy in our society needs thoughtful and just resolution.

In one vision of an enlightened multicultural society, no cultures would dominate others. Many vital cultures could thrive and all individuals could retain their culture of origin, if they so choose, as well as incorporate aspects of other cultures into their lives. In such a society all borders would be voluntary.

Literature and lessons centered around the concept of borders are presented to help students:

- Recognize that there are various kinds of borders in our society and understand that people on different sides of a border may see life differently.

- Understand their own feelings about borders in their lives.

- Promote curiosity about and respect for life in non-familiar cultures.

LESSON I
POEM: THE ENTICEMENT OF CROSSING A BORDER
based on "A Song in the Front Yard" by Gwendolyn Brooks

In this lesson students will write a poem about a person who finds life on the other side of a border to be "better" or more attractive than his or her own. The lesson is designed to encourage students to use concrete details that demonstrate the quality of the speaker's present life and evoke the appeal of life across the border.

Use "A Song in the Front Yard" to prompt a class discussion about the natural attraction to ways of life that are different from one's own. Pose some of the following questions to students:

- *Why does the speaker in the poem feel she lives a safe and sheltered life?*

- *What about the "back yard" fascinates the speaker?*

- *Which details, images, and metaphors provide clues about the speaker's current life? Which show the life the speaker wishes to have?*

PREWRITING
Guide students to choose a focus for their poems. Ask:

- *Who will be the speaker?*

- *What contrast will the speaker draw? Perhaps, as in Brooks's poem, life across the border seems wonderfully rough, wild, and free. On the other hand, the speaker may see life across the border as pleasantly safe, sheltered, or ordered.*

Explain to students that the subject of this assignment is broad, and there are a number of ways to approach writing about contrasting lifestyles. Remind students the speaker of the poem may reflect on life in the city, in the country, within a different ethnic group, or within a different socioeconomic group because it seems more wild, safe, interesting, fun, peaceful, or beautiful than his or her current life.

EXAMPLES OF POEM SUBJECTS

- *An academically oriented high school student wistfully contemplates the life of a student who is more sociable and goes to many parties (or vice versa).*

- *A person with a sedentary desk job thinks about how exciting it would be to fight fires, blaze trails, or build skyscrapers (or vice versa).*

- *A settled person longs for the life of a wanderer (or vice versa).*

- *A middle or high school student who spends much of his or her time on the street wishes for a safer, more middle-class lifestyle (or vice versa).*

- *A child who lives in the city imagines a better life in the country because there is nothing to do on a weekend in the city (or vice versa).*

- *An only child in a quiet house looks at the large extended family down the street and wishes he or she lived in a bustling house.*

- *A child in a bustling house longs for a peaceful home.*

Once students have chosen a focus for their poems, ask them to generate two lists of details that will help depict the speaker's current life and his or her fantasy. Encourage students to list more details than they will use. Then have students share their lists with two or three students, each of whom should add at least two details to the others' lists. One easy way to accomplish this sharing of ideas is to have students change seats two or three times and exchange lists with their new neighbors, generating two new ideas for each of them.

WRITING THE POEM

Have students review their lists and circle the ideas that best express the theme of the poem they wish to write. Suggest to students that they think of the sequence of the poem, writing lines that include many of the details in the list.

In Brooks's poem a middle-class girl imagines the freedom in the life of a girl from a poorer economic group. The following poem is an example of a poorer girl's look at a middle-class lifestyle.

SAMPLE

BALLET CASE

After school, when the cold winter light fades,
I sweep through the city with my ragged crowd.
Grab one candy bar and half a tuna sandwich for dinner, and kiss my
boyfriend under the streetlight. Tired, I make my way home, fall

asleep watching T.V. with my brother and two sisters, the day another
jangled chord.

I want to be a girl who steps out of a solid brick house on a snowy
day, my ballet shoes and leotard in a pink leather case, me . . . all
bundled and warm.
My friend would point, "Look at you schoolgirl. What are you doing
with that funny pink suitcase?"
I would say, "It's not bad: As and Bs, drama club, and ballet
class. It's fine to know that I'll have some sweet things. This
afternoon, I'll have my friends to my house (you too) for oranges,
cakes, and tea, chocolate soda in tall glasses, and dates."

LESSON 2
LITERATURE JOURNAL: LIVING ON THE FRONTIER
based on "Sonrisas" by Pat Mora

This literature journal entry can also be the basis of a good class discussion, either in small groups or as a whole class.

In "Sonrisas," Mora writes about her impressions of two sides of a
border. Ask students to respond in their journals or in discussion to the
following questions suggested by "Sonrisas":

- *Do you ever feel like you are in a borderland or frontier in which you don't really fit
  into either side? If so, describe the situations in which this feeling occurs.*

- *What are the borders you perceive?*

- *Are there borders within your school, community, family, or place of work?*

- *What can you do about this situation?*

- *What do you wish other people would do?*

- *Do you feel comfortable on both sides of one or more borders?*

- *Have you felt at ease on both sides of a border in the past, for instance as a young child?*

- *Can you communicate easily with people of different ethnic groups, socioeconomic
  groups, ages, genders, or cliques?*

- *To what factors do you attribute your success?*

- *Tell some stories about how you pass from one group to another.*

- *Do people notice your gift for communicating with many different people? How do they react?*

- *Do you enjoy being a cultural traveler?*

- *Do you notice that other people pass over borders easily and can communicate well with people of different cultures? Describe how they do this.*

- *Do you wish that you could cross borders more easily? Explain.*

LESSON 3
LITERATURE JOURNAL: A CHARACTER LOOKS AT BOTH SIDES OF A BORDER

SUGGESTED WORKS FROM *HEAR MY VOICE*
Any of the selections in the Borders unit
Family Dinner, page 77
From *Children of the River*, page 83
From *Donald Duk*, page 292

SUGGESTED LONGER WORKS
More Than Meets the Eye, Jeanne Betancourt
Donald Duk, Frank Chin
Coyotes, Ted Conover
Children of the River, Linda Crew
Migrant Souls, Arturo Islas
The War Between the Classes, Gloria D. Miklowitz
Clover, Dori Sanders
The Changelings, Jo Sinclair

1. Have students choose a character from a work in this anthology or one of the suggested books. Instruct students to use the first-person voice in the character's words to describe an important part of life on his or her side of a cultural border. Tell students the description can be of something typical, sad, funny, unjust, or something they like or don't like about life on their side of the border; it may be something the character would want readers to know, or it may be private. Also tell students that what they write about may relate to an actual part of the selected literature, or it may be about something they think could happen within the life of the character.

2. Have students present the same character's perceptions of people and events on the other side of the border, expressing the inner thoughts of the character and, if possible, using his or her actual words from the story or poem. Ask students:

- *Does the character think the people on the other side of the border are strange, funny, mean, ignorant, snobby, or scary? What other qualities do the people have?*

- *What does the character think happens on the other side of the border?*

3. Now have students reverse this process by presenting the point of view of a character on the other side of the border. This activity will encourage them to explore a less developed characterization, such as Bonna in "Seventh Grade."

LESSON 4
LITERATURE JOURNAL: LISTENING TO DIFFERENT DIALECTS

Dialects and accents in the United States are often associated with ethnic or class diversity. At "linguistic borders" people sometimes view each other with interest, appreciation, or admiration, and at other times with mocking and contempt. When people perceive that others view negatively their manner of speaking, they may internalize such negative views and subsequently suffer diminished self-esteem. This lesson and the four that follow help students develop an appreciation and understanding of the variety of dialects used in English speech and writing.

As students become acquainted with some of the speech patterns in the United States, you may want students to hear authentic representations of the dialects. If possible, invite to class members of the community, including parents, school staff, poets, and local performers, who speak different dialects of English. Ask the guests to read some of the selections from the anthology to the class.

SUGGESTED WORKS FROM *HEAR MY VOICE*
Who Said We All Have to Talk Alike, page 7
I'll Crack Your Head Kotsun, page 34
"Mommy, What Does 'Nigger' Mean?" page 45
From *Children of The River*, page 83
The Lesson, page 216
They Say Them Child Brides Don't Last, page 257

SUGGESTED LONGER WORKS
*I Know Why the Caged Bird Sings, Maya Angelou
*Their Eyes Were Watching God, Zora Neale Hurston
*Typical American, Gish Jen
Mama Day, Gloria Naylor
Huckleberry Finn, Mark Twain
*Macho! Victor Villasenor
The Color Purple, Alice Walker

1. Have students choose and then photocopy or copy in their literary journals three or four favorite passages from one of the works listed that contain narrative in dialect. Ask students to explain exactly what they like about the language in the passages. If you wish, guide students with the following questions:

- *Which words do you think are particularly interesting? Why?*

- *Do you find a certain humor or beauty in the language?*

- *Is the language clear and direct?*

- *Do you like the grammatical structure?*

- *Are sentences constructed in an interesting way?*

- *Do you like the sound of the speech?*

2. Ask students to "translate" the passages they chose into "standard" English. After they have completed their "translations," have students read them aloud in small groups. Then ask students to discuss in their groups what conversation would be like if everyone spoke standard English all the time. Do the members of the small groups carry on conversations in which they all speak in the same manner, pronounce words in the same way, and describe objects in similar ways? Ask students to consider why there are so many English dialects and what are some of the ways they use dialect in their daily lives.

LESSON 5
AUTOBIOGRAPHICAL ESSAY: WAYS OF SPEAKING
based on "Who Said We All Have to Talk Alike"

In this lesson students will explore their thoughts and feelings about linguistic diversity by sharing stories about dialects, accents, learning, and teaching "standard" English.

QUESTIONS FOR LITERATURE JOURNAL

- *If you were the mother, would you also have fired Neffie? Explain.*

- *What was your response to Neffie's accent and dialect? Explain.*

- *How does Neffie feel about her own way of speaking?*

- *Why does the mother feel so strongly about keeping her children from learning this new dialect? What does Neffie's accent mean to the mother?*

PREWRITING

As you read the following prompts aloud, have students write them in their journals so they can later jot their ideas under each one. The prompts are broad enough so each student will have sufficient material about which to write. The topics might be very personal and possibly painful for some students, so be particularly sensitive to students who choose not to share their writing.

To break the ice, I begin by talking about my experiences. I tell students how my mother tried to train me out of my New York accent and that my parents actually made fun of the way some of my friends talked. "Weyes Lawrie," (instead of "Where is Laurie") my mother would mock by exaggeration. This was unbearably embarrassing for me and it made me angry.

I continue reminiscing with my students about my early days in graduate school: When I spoke, I could still hear my voice with its traces of the dreaded accent. I constantly feared it would pop out and spoil the image I had created for myself. I also recount with chagrin how my friends and I began to mock the dialect of the natives of Pittsburgh, where I attended graduate school.

- *Has anyone ever corrected or ridiculed your accent or way of pronouncing words? For instance, have you been corrected by a parent or teacher for speaking with a Brooklyn or Chicano accent, a Midwestern "twang," or a black dialect? Have you ever been told not to use your first language? Have you ever been told to eliminate "foreign" words or phrases from your speech?*
  Describe these incidents. What happened exactly? What had you said? Who corrected you? What attitudes or feelings did the person express to you? How did you feel about the correction? What did you do about it?

- *Have you ever been corrected for the grammar of your dialect? What are the words or phrases you used?*

- *Do you like the way you speak? What especially do you like about it? What are some examples of words, phrases, and sounds you and people you know use? Do other people pick up on them and incorporate them into their speech?*

- *Have you ever been embarrassed by the way you, your family, or your friends speak? What in particular embarrasses you? In what situations do you tend to get embarrassed? What do you do about it?*

- *Do you like how other ways of speaking sound? What are some examples of words and phrases that you like? Why? Have you ever tried to pick up some words or ways of pronouncing words used by other people? If so, what are examples of phrases or pronunciations you have incorporated into your speech?*

- *Have you ever mocked the accents and dialects of others? When? What were the circumstances? What did you make fun of? How did the other person feel? How did you feel?*

Facilitate sharing these notes as much as possible to help students remember their experiences and generate more writing ideas.

WRITING THE FIRST DRAFT

Have students write autobiographical essays about their experiences with languages and dialects. Suggest they use their responses to the prompts as the basis of the essays. Urge students to use actual examples of speech and write about their experiences in as much detail as they can. Instruct them to summarize their experiences with language and dialect into a few focused points in the introduction and conclusion. Remind students to use prewriting notes as well as class discussion to help recall details.

LESSON 6
BILINGUAL ACROSTIC POEM

This lesson and the following two lessons engage students in writing bilingual poetry. There are a number of reasons for having students write bilingual poetry:

- To publicly acknowledge and use the skill of those students who are bilingual. Because language is an important part of a person's identity, recognition of their skills can be a great self-esteem boost for bilingual students.

- To demonstrate the expressive qualities of various languages.

- To create uniquely evocative poetry. Bilingual poetry is one example of how elements of different cultures can combine to create something beautiful and unique.

- Lessons on bilingual poetry provide an excellent opportunity to use the skills of bilingual community members, including parents, school staff, poets, and performers. Sending home a letter early in the year requesting help in bilingual projects from all those who speak languages other than English may also help involve more parents in school life.

- Students from advanced English as a Second Language and foreign language classes can also serve as linguistic experts. The teacher does not have to know any of the languages used, but must be a willing learner.

The following simple form will allow students to concentrate on using the words of a language or dialect other than standard English. Ask students to follow the instructions listed below:

1. *Write your (or someone else's) name vertically. Use the successive letters of the name to begin each line of the poem. The entire poem should be about the person named.*

2. *Add interest to the poem by varying the length of the lines and breaking lines in mid-sentence.*

3. *Use at least three words from a language or dialect other than standard English.*

4. *Write your first draft in English, and make notes about which words you want to translate into another language, or use non-English expressions in your first draft.*

5. *Make your final choices of non-English words and phrases for your poem and translate them into English for the footnotes.*

Ask bilingual students or bilingual guests from the community to act as translation consultants. I like to work as a class, calling on students one by one as they ask how to express their ideas in another language. When we discover the answers, I write the translations on the board.

Having a variety of dictionaries in the room during the lesson is also helpful. Students can use the dictionaries as their resource if there are no bilingual students or community members to help. If you are using only the dictionaries, I suggest that the class break into groups to look up words and concentrate on one or two languages.

SAMPLE BILINGUAL ACROSTIC POEM

LAUREN/LIBBY

Libby is my Jewish nomen.[1]
Although I rarely
Use it, I
Return to Yiddish[2] in my thoughts. After all,
English can't translate, "So,
Nu?"[3]

LESSON 7

BILINGUAL POEM: ASPECTS OF A PLACE
based on "Chicago" by Carl Sandberg

In one of his most famous poems, Carl Sandberg wrote about the vibrant midwestern city of Chicago. In this project students will write a poem about a place of their choice modeled on the poem "Chicago." They

---

Words from the Yiddish language:
1. nomen—name
2. Yiddish—a language written in the Hebrew alphabet with vocabulary from Hebrew, Russian, Polish, English, and other languages which is spoken by Eastern European Jews and their descendants in other countries
3. So nu?—What's up? What's happening?

might add particular interest to their poems by featuring a place in which at least one other language besides English is spoken and by using ten or more words from one of these languages to help evoke the atmosphere of the place.

1. Have students analyze the poem "Chicago" by responding to the following questions:

- *What is the function of the first four lines?*

- *What is happening in the lines that begin with "They tell me"?*

- *How does the speaker answer in each of these lines?*

- *What does the speaker say to "give back the sneer"?*

- *To what is the city of Chicago compared?*

- *What overall impression of Chicago does this speaker give?*

2. Ask students to draw lines around the main sections of the poem.

3. Guide students in analyzing the tone of the poem. Ask them whether they find it sweet, bland, romantic, angry, argumentative, persuasive, etc. Have individual students read the poem aloud in what they feel is the appropriate tone. Ask students to identify the details the author uses to express his tone.

PREWRITING

4. Explain to students that rather than being a tedious chore, prewriting can make the actual writing of the poem much easier. Suggest they consider three or four places to write about where a language other than standard English is spoken. Tell students the places may be continents, countries, areas, states, cities, neighborhoods, schools, classrooms, homes, and so forth, and that they may wish to consult maps to get ideas of places about which to write. Provide the following model to help students generate ideas about their choices:

SAMPLE PREWRITING

PLACE
New York City

NEGATIVE ASPECT
- *dirty/smoggy/has foul air*

Details
- *Most days you cannot see the skyline from the East River.*
- *The smog burns your eyes and lungs.*
- *Many people have a constant sore throat.*

NEGATIVE ASPECT
- *overcrowded*

Details
- *You cannot find a seat on public transportation.*
- *At stores, like supermarkets, to check out you have to wait for 10 or 15 minutes.*
- *Lines for first-run movies circle the block.*

NEGATIVE ASPECT
- *expensive*

Details
- *Movies cost $7.50.*
- *A modest apartment costs $1000/month.*

POSITIVE ASPECT
- *The city is vibrant.*

Details
- *You can walk down streets at night and find that many stores and restaurants are open at a time most other cities are shut down.*
- *Streets are filled with people who express themselves dramatically; people argue, joke, and complain with flair.*

POSITIVE ASPECT
- *The city is famous for its entertainment.*

Details
- *There are music clubs for all kinds of jazz, classical, and popular music.*
- *There are concerts, parks, museums, galleries, libraries; Broadway, Off-Broadway, and even Off-Off Broadway; countless movie theaters, including experimental ones; art in the streets, such as mime, circus acts, and musical groups.*

POSITIVE ASPECT
- *The city is international.*

Details

- *People from all nations bring to New York City their food and their music. In Central Park on a Sunday afternoon you can see Russian dancers and Caribbean congo drummers. You can eat in a variety of restaurants, such as Russian, Jewish, Ethiopian, Northern Italian, German, Salvadoran, Hawaiian, Haitian, and Peruvian.*

METAPHORS/PERSONIFICATIONS ABOUT THE PLACE

- *The city is a loud, exciting community.*
- *The city is a rich, earthy tapestry.*
- *New York is the "Troy" of the United States, city built upon city.*
- *New York is a dramatic actor, comfortable with a variety of sets, clothing, accents, and moods.*

WRITING THE FIRST DRAFT

5. Direct students to use the form of "Chicago" in their own poems to the degree that it fits their purpose. Review with them that the model form contains:

- *a brief, strong description of a place*

- *a series of statements giving the popularly held negative views about the place with admissions of their truth*

- *a strong counterargument showing the positive features of the place*

- *a summary using metaphors and personifications of the place.*

Remind students the goal is to use the poem as a scaffold to help find their own ideas and details.

Early in the process of writing the first draft, provide plenty of opportunity for students to find out how to express their ideas in other languages. This can be a particularly enjoyable part of the activity. As described in Lesson 6, I like to conduct the linguistic consultation as a class. I create a glossary on the board that lasts for the duration of the project.

Linguistic discoveries students make while producing the glossary deepen their respect for the expressive power of different languages. Students ask, for instance: "How do you say 'boring' in Spanish?" "How do you say 'mellow' in Spanish?" On the board go the translations: 'boring' is *aburrido* and 'mellow' is *maduro*. We pause to discuss nuances of one language that don't quite get translated into the other. For example, *maduro* comes from the verb *madurar*, which means "to ripen" as well as "to think out." So a mellow atmosphere can be seen as ripe.

6. After students choose which non-English expressions to use, editing groups or pairs can be formed so students can help each other with tone, structure, details, and mechanics in their second and third drafts.

STUDENTS EVALUATE THE ACTIVITY IN LETTERS TO THE TEACHER

7. Ask students to write letters about what they learned from writing the poetry. Ask them:

- *How did you feel about learning from other students?*

- *How did you feel about teaching other students?*

- *What did you think about having people from the community help the class with bilingual poetry?*

PUBLISHING

8. Completed works can be published in a variety of ways. You may wish to compile a magazine or class book or host a party for parents and other community members at which students read their poems.

ADDITIONAL OPPORTUNITIES FOR WRITING BILINGUAL POETRY IN THIS GUIDE

- Poem: Going Home, Family and Generations, Lesson 2, page 36

- Poem: An Ancestral Perspective, Family and Generations, Lesson 4, page 38

- Poems: Cinquains about the Americas, Society: Conflict, Struggle, and Change, Lesson 3, page 56.

- Poem in Two Voices: Ancestral Roots, Personal Identity, Lesson 1, page 75.

- Poem: Reflection on a Food, Celebrations, Lesson 5, page 90.

LESSON 8

MULTICULTURAL BOOK BRIGADE: OLDER STUDENTS WRITE BOOKS
RECOGNIZING AND CELEBRATING DIVERSITY FOR A YOUNGER AUDIENCE

A number of teachers have developed lessons in which older students write books for a younger audience. The lesson that follows was designed by Michelann Ortloff of Portland, Oregon. I have given Michelann's Book Brigade a multicultural focus.

The process of writing children's books gives high school students the opportunity to examine and put into practice the concepts of plot, character, theme, tone, purpose, and audience. The end products are beautiful books that young children love to have read to them. High school students can provide wonderful role models for younger children. In turn, the high school students' self-esteem is enhanced when they care for and teach children. You will find that even very reluctant high school writers are successful in this activity.

In the multicultural book brigade high school students have an opportunity to deepen their understanding and appreciation of cultural diversity by writing, illustrating, and reading aloud their own children's books, which will include themes that help break down stereotypes, prejudice, and intolerance, replacing these with historical facts and affirmations of different cultures.

PROCEDURE

This project takes at least ten sessions of a one-hour class.

1. Read some examples of children's books to your class. Display a varied sample of great children's literature around your room.

2. Ask students to share their favorite childhood books and authors. List these titles and names on the board. High school students may remember many books and authors from their own childhoods with great fondness.

3. As a class, list characteristics of the most commonly cited books.

4. Introduce the concept of audience so students will think about the age group for which they are writing. Related to audience, discuss the different purposes their books can have, for instance, making kids laugh, creating suspense, or teaching particular lessons. When dis-

cussing purposes of children's books and your students' personal favorites, emphasize the fantasy, magic, and humor that is a key part of literature for young people. When students write their own books, they will want to entertain as well as teach.

5. Read aloud and analyze the plots of selected children's books. In a discussion of what makes a plot interesting, show how authors vary the intensity of the action so they do not give away the whole story at once. Michelann Ortloff uses graph paper to map out the changes in intensity within a story.

   As a class, graph the plot of a children's book on the chalkboard or overhead projector by breaking the story into the major events (listed along the x-axis) and estimating the "intensity rating" (the y value) of each event. After doing this as a class have students, perhaps in pairs, choose two or three books to graph. Post and discuss the graphs.

6. Read another book to the class, this time emphasizing character. Discuss the personalities of the characters. Also look for problems or complications of plot that confront the main character, and consider whether and how the main characters change. Have pairs of students choose two or three books to analyze for character.

   The analyses should contain a description of the character's personality. Have students support their judgments about the character's personality with details about what the character says and does. The analyses should consider the main problems the character faces as well as any changes within the character. Discuss a number of these analyses as a class.

7. Take ample time to read aloud some children's books that break down stereotypes and prejudice. Such stories are often wonderfully subtle and provide excellent models for writing. Ask the class to explain the lesson(s) of each book. For example, prize-winning *Ben's Trumpet* by Rachel Isadora depicts the rich cultural heritage African Americans have brought to jazz. The strong, protective black male in the story is, in addition, a positive role model. *Flossie And The Fox* is a children's book about an African-American girl outsmarting a fox. This story successfully breaks down stereotypes of African Americans and girls in one entertaining tale.

The following is a list of outstanding children's books with special emphasis on those that help replace stereotypes and prejudice with acceptance, historical accuracy, and celebration. (For a complete bibliography of children's books that present a culturally-aware perspective, write to Cooperative Children's Book Center, 4290 Helen C. White Hall, University of Wisconsin, 600 N. Park Street, Madison, Wisconsin 53706. Ask for the bibliography by Kruse and Horning.)

Bang, Molly. *The Paper Crane.* New York: Mulberry Books, 1987.

Retold and illustrated by Tomie De Paola. *The Legend of the Indian Paintbrush.* New York: G.P. Putnam and Sons, 1988.

Everett, Louise. *Amigo Means Friend.* Mahwah, NJ: Troll Associates, a subsidiary of Educational Reading Services, 1988.

Garcia, Richard. *My Aunt Otilia's Spirits: Los Espiritus de Mi Tia Otilia.* San Francisco: Children's Book Press, 1987.

Hoffman, Mary. *Amazing Grace.* New York: Dial Books for Young Readers, Penguin Books U.S.A., 1991.

White Deer of Autumn (Gabriel Horn). *The Great Change.* Hillsboro, OR: Beyond Words Publishing, Inc., 1992.

Kimmel, Eric. *Hershel and the Hanukkah Goblins.* New York: Holiday House, Inc., 1989.

Levine, Ellen. *I Hate English!* New York: Scholastic Press, 1989.

Polacco, Patricia. *Boat Ride with Lillian Two Blossom.* New York: Philomel Books, The Putnam and Grosset Book Group, 1988.

— *Chicken Sunday.* New York: Philomel Books, The Putnam and Grosset Book Group, 1992.

— *Mrs. Katz and Tush.* New York: Bantam Little Rooster, Bantam Books, 1992.

Prusski, Jeffrey. *Bring Back the Deer.* San Diego, CA: Gulliver Books, Harcourt Brace Jovanovich, Inc., 1988.

Ringgold, Faith. *Aunt Harriet.* New York: Crown Publishing, a division of Random House, 1993.

—————————. *Tar Beach.* New York: Crown Publishing, a division of Random House, 1992.

Rodriguez, Anita. *Jamal and the Angel.* New York: Clarkson N. Potter, Inc., a member of Crown Publishing Group, 1992.

Rohmer, Harriet. *Mr. Sugar Came to Town/La Visita del Señor Azucar.* San Francisco: Children's Book Press, 1989.

Rylant, Cynthia. *Appalachia: The Voices of Sleeping Birds.* San Diego, CA: Harcourt Brace Jovanovich, Inc. 1991.

Sakai, Kimiko. *Sachiko Means Happiness.* San Francisco: Children's Book Press, 1990.

Say, Allen. *El Chino.* Boston: Houghton Mifflin Co., 1990.

Sonneborn, Ruth. *Friday Night is Papa Night.* New York: Puffin Books, a division of Penguin Books, 1987.

Tan, Amy. *The Moon Lady.* New York: Macmillan Publishing Company, 1992.

Yarbrough, Camille. *Cornrows.* New York: Sandcastle Books, Putnam Publishing Group, 1992.

Yashima, Taro. *Umbrella.* New York: Viking Press, 1958.

8. As a class, discuss possible topics, plots, and themes for students' books, emphasizing that it is possible to express a theme in a very subtle manner. Possible themes and topics include:

- *If other people make fun of a person's dialect, skin color, or clothing style, what should you do?*

- *Ignorance about people from a different culture may lead to contempt or prejudice.*

- *Just because someone is poor does not mean he or she is not talented, smart, or creative.*

- *What is it like to be different from everyone else in a group?*

- *An openness to someone else's culture can lead to pleasant surprises.*

- *What if there were no prejudice?*

- *How can kids change the prejudice of adults?*

- *What if everyone were the same?*

- *Who are some heroes and heroines of different cultures?*

- *What if you could switch places for one month with someone from a different culture?*

- *How do people of different cultures cooperate to achieve a goal?*

- *What might someone learn from a person of a different culture?*

- *Create a story based on an historical event.*

- *Create a story based on a notable person's life.*

- *Develop a plot that explains a tradition of a certain culture.*

9. At this point students should finalize decisions about their audience and purpose, and focus on plot, characters, and theme. As I mentioned above, the beauty of children's literature is the degree of fantasy, magic, and humor that can be used to express important themes. Encourage your students to really tap into what children would like. They should use the model children's books for ideas and suggestions.

   You may wish to prepare "brainstorming sheets" for students to help them focus on their choices of plot, character, and theme. Some students may find it easier to begin by focusing on characters, their names, physical characteristics, and personalities, while others may prefer to begin by developing the plot. Share results of brainstorming with the entire class so those having a harder time getting started will have hints.

   Remind students not to give the plot away all at once, but to build to a climax. Also encourage ample use of dialogue and description of action both to move the plot along and describe the characters' personalities.

10. Schedule time for teacher-student and peer conferences to help generate ideas as students write their first drafts.

11. After drafting, editing, and typing or printing the manuscript, students will be ready to illustrate their stories. Survey with the class a

variety of illustration styles. Some are realistic, others are more abstract and stylized. When illustrating their books, some students may wish to consult with others for advice and help.

12. Students should practice reading the books aloud to the class, making a special effort to speak in a voice that can be easily understood and to use eye contact.

13. Take a field trip to an elementary school. It is best to make early arrangements with a number of teachers in the grade school so that all students have a chance to read their books to three or four classes. Enjoy!

LESSON 9
LOGO DESIGN/DIARY ENTRY: SCHOOL SUBCULTURES VIEWED POSITIVELY

The objectives of this lesson are:

- To increase awareness of the different cultures within the school and in the larger society.

- To be able to describe other cultures without negative stereotyping.

1. Have the entire class participate in making a list of the different subcultures in the school. Have small groups of students tour the school and the schoolgrounds and construct maps that indicate borders and subcultures. In many high schools, groups may include students who see themselves primarily as academic or athletic or musical. Some students may identify with football, basketball, drama, science, heavy metal music, hip-hop music, or reggae. Other students may identify with an ethnic group. If students label a group in a way that can be interpreted pejoratively, like "druggies," encourage a more neutral label. If appropriate, have students label groups according to where they hang out in the school.

2. Ask small groups to draw or use magazine pictures to make logos for the different subcultures that members of the subcultures themselves approve of. Encourage students to design the logos to express as much pride and respect as possible.

3. Post and discuss the logos. Discuss how they differ from the common negative stereotypes. Guide students to talk about why people some-

times judge other people negatively without really knowing them or the circumstances of their lives.

4. Have students write diary entries in the first person about either a typical day or an exciting day from the point of view of a student of a different subculture than their own. Ask students to interview members of that subculture in order to create realistic diary entries. Suggest to students some topics:

- *attitudes toward different subjects in school*

- *work outside school*

- *hobbies and activities after school*

- *styles of social gatherings*

- *problems*

- *goals for the future*

- *favorite music and bands*

- *who time is spent with*

- *what subjects are discussed between friends*

- *where time is spent between classes*

- *what issues arise during the school day*

~ ~

LOVE

*B*ECAUSE LOVE IS A UNIVERSAL HUMAN EMOTION, the literary works and projects in this section can help break down previously learned stereo-types and enable students to appreciate common traits of human nature.

LESSON 1
POEM: AN ENCHANTING DATE
based on "Juke Box Love Song" by Langston Hughes

ANALYZE "JUKE BOX LOVE SONG"

Have students list the sensory images of Harlem Hughes employs to describe a festive night out.

PREWRITING

Have students create a list of sensory images of their own neighborhood, city, town, or region that might be part of a romantic encounter or date. Direct students to include in their lists more details than they will use in their poems.

A sample prewriting list for a love poem using images of Portland, Oregon, might include: lush greenery, bountiful flowers, cream-colored roses, pastel rhododendrons, daphnes whose fragrance travels half a block in the early spring, camellias, evergreens in the mist, long summer days, dewy grasses, converging rivers, bridges lit at night.

Ask students to share their three favorite images with the class. Copy them on the board, a chart, or transparency so that everyone in the class will have a substantial list for their poems.

WRITING

Have students write a love poem from one person to another describing an enchanting date, using details from the list generated by the class. Ask students to consider the following questions:

- *Where do you go?*

- *What do you do?*

- *Are you and your date outdoors?*

- *What time of day is it?*

- *What season is it?*

- *Are you describing an urban or rural scene?*

- *Is there music? What kind? How does it make you feel?*

- *Do you eat lunch or dinner? Where?*

SAMPLE POEM

RIVER LOVE SONG

I could take the long Oregon summer's night
and put you under
its sky.
Take you out on the moon covered river in a little boat
to let the water be our music.
Let the fragrance of roses be our perfume, and the lit bridges
be our swooping fancy roof.

LESSON 2
EXCHANGE OF LETTERS BETWEEN LITERARY CHARACTERS IN THE SAME WORK

SUGGESTED WORKS FROM *HEAR MY VOICE*
all selections in the Love unit

SUGGESTED LONGER WORKS
*If Beale Street Could Talk, James Baldwin
*More than Meets the Eye, Jeanne Betancourt
Jane Eyre, Charlotte Brönte
Wuthering Heights, Emily Brönte
*Eat a Bowl of Tea, Louis Chu
*Children of the River, Linda Crew
Madame Bovary, Gustave Flaubert

A White Romance, Virginia Hamilton
Jude The Obscure, Thomas Hardy
Tess of the D'Urbervilles, Thomas Hardy
A Farewell to Arms, Ernest Hemingway
For Whom the Bell Tolls, Ernest Hemingway
Their Eyes Were Watching God, Zora Neale Hurston
West Side Story, Arthur Laurents
Thousand Pieces of Gold, Ruthanne L. McCunn
Beloved, Toni Morrison
Mama Day, Gloria Naylor
Cyrano De Bergerac, Edmond Rostand
Antony and Cleopatra, William Shakespeare
Romeo and Juliet, William Shakespeare
Pygmalion, George Bernard Shaw
Fiddler on the Roof, Joseph Stein
Anna Karenina, Leo Tolstoy

Have students write love letters between characters from one of the selections listed. Suggest they use their knowledge of the characters, setting, and plot to provide a realistic setting for the letters, giving clues, for example, about the stage of the relationship in which these letters are written.

- *Are the characters just getting to know each other?*

- *Are they just falling in love?*

- *Have they been in love for years?*

Remind students that in "Anniversary," "Finding a Wife," "Never Offer Your Heart to Someone Who Eats Hearts," "The Pieces," and "When Your Eyes Speak," readers meet one of the lovers indirectly through the main speaker. Students may be interested in giving this "silent" person the voice to speak out in a letter.

Suggest to students they explain all or some of the following in the letters:

- *Why are these characters communicating by letter?*

- *Are they apart?*

- *Are there problems in their relationship? If so, why?*

- *Do they have to keep their love secret? Why?*

- *How does their relationship affect other aspects of their lives?*

Urge students to go beyond the plot by making up new details about the future while demonstrating their understanding of the work. Also guide students to capture the specific tone of the relationship and to incorporate into the letters words and phrases that the characters actually use in the story.

LESSON 3
EXCHANGE OF LETTERS ABOUT LOVE BETWEEN CHARACTERS IN DIFFERENT WORKS

SUGGESTED WORKS FROM *HEAR MY VOICE*
all selections in the Love unit

SUGGESTED LONGER WORKS
*If Beale Street Could Talk, James Baldwin
*More than Meets the Eye, Jeanne Betancourt
Jane Eyre, Charlotte Brönte
Wuthering Heights, Emily Brönte
*Eat a Bowl of Tea, Louis Chu
*Children of the River, Linda Crew
Madame Bovary, Gustave Flaubert
*A White Romance, Virginia Hamilton
Jude The Obscure, Thomas Hardy
Tess of the D'Urbervilles, Thomas Hardy
A Farewell to Arms, Ernest Hemingway
For Whom the Bell Tolls, Ernest Hemingway
*Their Eyes Were Watching God, Zora Neale Hurston
West Side Story, Arthur Laurents
Mama Day, Gloria Naylor
Cyrano De Bergerac, Edmond Rostand
Antony and Cleopatra, William Shakespeare
Romeo and Juliet, William Shakespeare
Pygmalion, George Bernard Shaw
Fiddler on the Roof, Joseph Stein
Anna Karenina, Leo Tolstoy

Ask students to create a series of letters in which characters from two of the works listed above write to one another about the joys, tribulations, and mysteries of love. Encourage students to go beyond the actual events in the literary works as long as they remain true to what is plausible for the characters. If students need help getting started, you may want to present some of the following suggestions for the contents of the letter:

- *a character's inner thoughts about his or her loved one*

- *the problems of the relationship*

- *doubts or hopes about the relationship*

- *questions or observations about his or her correspondent's relationship*

Next, have students write a letter in which the character from the second work responds to the first letter.

Varied perspectives on love and the experiences of the characters should emerge in these letters. For instance, the speaker in "Finding A Wife," who is presumably the author Gary Soto, might ask Romeo from *Romeo and Juliet* if he ever worries that he and Juliet are merely infatuated with each other. Soto may relate how it took him some time to find out that his relationship with Carolyn was serious. Romeo and Soto might philosophize in their letters about the probability of love at first sight.

Juliet from *Romeo and Juliet* might write to the young woman in "Family Dinner" that she wishes she could bring her boyfriend home to her parents. She may also say, however, that the secrecy of her relationship with Romeo makes their feelings more intense.

VARIATION: PERSONAL CORRESPONDENCE ABOUT LOVE WITH A LITERARY CHARACTER

Ask students to pretend they are friends with a character from one of the selections listed above and to write a series of letters between themselves and this character about their experiences, questions, and thoughts about love. Suggest that students include their observations about this character's relationships. For instance, they might respond to the speaker in "The Pieces" when she asks if a heart can be mended once it is broken.

LESSON 4

CHARACTERS PRESENT GIFTS TO EACH OTHER

SUGGESTED WORKS FROM *HEAR MY VOICE*
all selections in the Love unit

SUGGESTED LONGER WORKS
If Beale Street Could Talk, James Baldwin
More than Meets the Eye, Jeanne Betancourt
Jane Eyre, Charlotte Brontë
Wuthering Heights, Emily Brontë
Eat a Bowl of Tea, Louis Chu
Children of the River, Linda Crew
Madame Bovary, Gustave Flaubert
A White Romance, Virginia Hamilton
Jude The Obscure, Thomas Hardy
Tess of the D'Urbervilles, Thomas Hardy
A Farewell to Arms, Ernest Hemingway
For Whom the Bell Tolls, Ernest Hemingway
Their Eyes Were Watching God, Zora Neale Hurston
West Side Story, Arthur Laurents
Beloved, Toni Morrison
Mama Day, Gloria Naylor
Cyrano De Bergerac, Edmond Rostand
Antony and Cleopatra, William Shakespeare
Romeo and Juliet, William Shakespeare
Pygmalion, George Bernard Shaw
Fiddler on the Roof, Joseph Stein
Anna Karenina, Leo Tolstoy

Have students draw or find magazine photos of items that characters from two or more of the works listed might give to their beloved. Ask students to consider the occasion of the present and to use details from the story and knowledge of the characters to help them make realistic choices.

After students have chosen their images, ask them to explain why they chose their particular gifts. For example, the speaker in the poem "Anniversary" by Judith Ortiz Cofer might give her husband a beautiful blank book so they can write together about their relationship and record their thinking about the state of the country and the world over the years they have known each other.

LESSON 5
ILLUSTRATING FAVORITE SCENES

SUGGESTED WORKS FROM *HEAR MY VOICE*
all selections in the Love unit

Have students draw or find magazine photos that depict their favorite scenes from the stories in this section. Have the rest of the class guess which story and which specific part of the story the picture illustrates.

LESSON 6
ANALYTICAL ESSAY: LOVE ACROSS BORDERS

SUGGESTED WORKS FROM *HEAR MY VOICE*
Family Dinner, page 77
From *Children of the River,* page 83
She Is Beautiful in Her Whole Being, page 94
Finding A Wife, page 117

SUGGESTED LONGER WORKS
*More Than Meets the Eye, Jeanne Betancourt
Jane Eyre, Charlotte Brönte
*Children of the River, Linda Crew
*A White Romance, Virginia Hamilton
West Side Story, Arthur Laurents
Romeo and Juliet, William Shakespeare
Fiddler on the Roof, Joseph Stein

In this lesson, students will use their own experience and observations of others, as well as insights gained from some of the works in this section and related literature to analyze issues common among relationships across borders. Encourage students to use specific details from literature and their own lives to support their points.

PROMPTS

- *What are some complications that can arise in a romantic relationship when people come from two sides of a border? Can the complications intensify emotions? How?*

- *Can obstacles prove too difficult to deal with? How?*

- *Can misunderstandings arise from differences of background? Explain.*

- *Can a relationship be strengthened because of differences in cultural background? How?*

LESSON 7
ILLUSTRATING A LOVE POEM

SUGGESTED WORKS FROM *HEAR MY VOICE*
Juke Box Love Song, page 81
Anniversary, page 115
Never Offer Your Heart to Someone Who Eats Hearts, page 120
The Pieces/Fragmentos, page 122
When Your Eyes Speak/Cuando Hablan Tus Ojos, page 123

Have students copy one of the poems listed above or another favorite poem on a large sheet of paper or posterboard. Then ask them to write a paragraph about the meaning of the poem or the reason they like it and to illustrate it with drawings or with photos from a magazine.

LESSON 8
ACROSTIC LOVE POEM

Have students write an acrostic love poem from one literary character to another using the letters of the character's name as the initial letters of each line. Ask students to demonstrate their understanding of the plot and the personalities of the characters and to attempt to reflect the tone of the work. Also urge them to incorporate into the poem some actual words and phrases of the character who is speaking. Remind students to vary the length of the lines in order to add interest to their poems.

SAMPLE ACROSTIC LOVE POEM

TO JULIET

Jewel in an Ethiop's ear, you hang upon the cheek of night.
Urgent
Love
Is what I feel. Waiting for parents to agree would be
Eternity.
Tonight!

LESSON 9
PERSONAL WRITING ON LOVE

SUGGESTED WORKS FROM *HEAR MY VOICE*
all selections in the Love unit

SUGGESTED LONGER WORKS
*If Beale Street Could Talk, James Baldwin
*More than Meets the Eye, Jeanne Betancourt
Jane Eyre, Charlotte Brönte
Wuthering Heights, Emily Brönte
*Eat a Bowl of Tea, Louis Chu
*Children of the River, Linda Crew
Madame Bovary, Gustave Flaubert
*A White Romance, Virginia Hamilton
Jude The Obscure, Thomas Hardy
Tess of the D'Urbervilles, Thomas Hardy
A Farewell to Arms, Ernest Hemingway
For Whom the Bell Tolls, Ernest Hemingway
*Their Eyes Were Watching God, Zora Neale Hurston
West Side Story, Arthur Laurents
Mama Day, Gloria Naylor
Cyrano De Bergerac, Edmond Rostand
Antony and Cleopatra, William Shakespeare
Romeo and Juliet, William Shakespeare
Pygmalion, George Bernard Shaw
Fiddler on the Roof, Joseph Stein
Anna Karenina, Leo Tolstoy

Have students write in their journals about a character from one of the selections on love with whom they closely identify. Ask students:

- *Does your identification rest on similarity of situation? Perhaps you have brought home a boyfriend or girlfriend from a different ethnic group as the young woman in "Family Dinner" does.*

- *Is your identification based on a similarity of personality characteristics? For instance, are you fun-loving and optimistic like Tea Cake in* Their Eyes Were Watching God?

Remind students to provide ample detail from their lives and the literature selection in their journal entries.

LESSON 10

ESSAY: THE TRANSFORMING QUALITIES OF LOVE

SUGGESTED WORKS FROM *HEAR MY VOICE*
From *Children of the River*, page 83
She Is Beautiful in Her Whole Being, page 94

SUGGESTED LONGER WORKS
Jane Eyre, Charlotte Brönte
West Side Story, Arthur Laurents
*Beloved, Toni Morrison
*Tell Me a Riddle, Tillie Olsen
Cyrano De Bergerac, Edmond Rostand
Romeo and Juliet, William Shakespeare
Spinoza of Market Street and Other Stories, Isaac Bashevis Singer

Ask students to choose a character from one of the works listed above who was transformed by falling in love or by being in love and to contrast traits of the character before and after he or she was in love. Instruct students to provide details and quotes to justify their positions. If students wish, they may expand their essay to address more than one character and more than one work.

LESSON 11

WRITE A SCENE ABOUT LOVERS FROM TWO FEUDING GROUPS
modeled on a scene from Romeo and Juliet

This lesson is for classes that are studying *Romeo and Juliet*.
In this lesson students will use *Romeo and Juliet* as a model to write a scene about lovers from two groups who are feuding with each other.

PREWRITING

1. Have students choose two lovers or friends from two groups who, like the Montagues and the Capulets, frequently clash. Tell students the groups may be real or fictional, and they may exist in the past, present, or future. For example, they may wish to write about a young man of the Lakota nation and a young woman pioneer, people from different

ethnic groups or different economic classes in a big city, or members of rival gangs or different high school cliques.

2. Ask students to generate ideas about the background of the groups and to describe some of the major battles. Have students who have based their scenes on fact research the feuding groups, while students who have made up the characters use their imaginations to develop the action of the scene. Ask:

- *Why did the groups begin to fight?*

- *Was it over small incidents?*

- *Is the feud ancient?*

- *Are their fights over economic turf?*

- *Is the feud about social or economic injustice?*

3. Now have students choose the scene from *Romeo and Juliet* they will use as their model, and guide them to begin to create their own versions. Suggest to students they use a scene that contains a variety of other characters along with Romeo and Juliet in order to vividly portray the feuding factions. Have students think about aspects of the major and minor characters: name, age, physical type, personality, social class, clothing. Also ask students to describe details of the setting that could set the appropriate mood.

You may wish to provide the following example:

> *If you were to model your scene on Act I, scene 5, which portrays Lord Capulet's party, you might show a young woman's father throwing some sort of gathering for his friends. What kind of party, music, food, dancing, decorations will you put in your version of this scene? In Shakespeare's scene, Romeo and his friends crash the party in hopes of seeing Romeo's original heartthrob. Shortly after Romeo's arrival to the party, Romeo and Juliet meet and fall in love. Tybalt, Juliet's cousin, flys into a rage when he recognizes Romeo, who is a Montague. In your version, exactly how do your characters meet? What do they say to each other? What do they do? Who plays the role of Tybalt and what exactly does he say and do? How do Juliet's parents react to the couple?*

Another scene from the play that involves a variety of characters from both sides of the feud is Act III, scene I.

4. As students write their first drafts, ask them to provide in parentheses stage directions and information for the actors. Suggest they put most of the plot content in the dialogue and action, rather than in long descriptions. Refer students to the text of *Romeo and Juliet* and other plays for models of this technique.

After students have finished editing and redrafting the manuscript, have them practice the scenes in small groups and perform them for the entire class.

These scenes can be written by groups, pairs, or individuals and performed by a group for the class.

✳ ✳ ✳ ✳ ✳ ✳ ✳ ✳ ✳ ✳ ✳ ✳ ✳ ✳ ✳ ✳ ✳

FAMILY AND GENERATIONS

*M*ANY EMOTIONS AND ISSUES surrounding family life and interactions among members of various generations are universal. Stories about families, like those about love, remind readers of the common issues and concerns of all people. By exploring their own and literary families, students engage in literature on a personal level.

LESSON I
LETTER TO THE EDITOR
based on From *A Bintel Brief*: Letters from the World of Our Fathers

SUGGESTED WORKS *FROM HEAR MY VOICE*
A Moving Day, page 135
The Bending of a Twig, page 145
Scribbles, page 153
I Stand Here Ironing, page 158

SUGGESTED LONGER WORKS
*How the Garcia Girls Lost Their Accents, Julia Alvarez
*Go Tell It on the Mountain, James Baldwin
*A Yellow Raft in Blue Water, Michael Dorris
*Love Medicine, Louise Erdrich
*Tracks, Louise Erdrich
*My Love, My Love, Rosa Gay
*Tell Me a Riddle, Tillie Olsen
The Chosen, Chaim Potok
*Clover, Dori Sanders
King Lear, William Shakespeare
*The Joy Luck Club, Amy Tan
*The Kitchen God's Wife, Amy Tan
Our Town, Thornton Wilder

Have students write a letter to the editor of *The Jewish Daily Forward* in the voice of a character from a literary work listed above about a problem this character has with a member of his or her family. Guide students to use their knowledge of the character and his or her situation to write openly about what this family member is doing that hurts, angers, disgusts, annoys, or embarrasses him or her.

VARIATION

Have students write their own letter to the editor of *The Jewish Daily Forward* in which they ask for advice about an actual problem with a family member.

LESSON 2

POEM: GOING HOME
based on "Poem Near Midway Truck Stop" by Lance Henson

Home is often significant for a variety of reasons. It is a familiar place, it is often a place where we experience life changes, and it is frequently associated with our family of origin. Lance Henson depicts a truck stop where he stops to sleep on his way home.

Have students write a poem about a person who is going back home and is at a resting stop along the way. The resting place may be a diner in Columbus, Ohio, a pizza parlor in Los Angeles, a rest stop on Interstate 80 outside Salt Lake City, Utah, or any other place that might be an appropriate setting for the poem.

Ask students whether the differences between home and the resting place are stark or whether there are some similarities between the places. For example, in Henson's poem, the rest stop is both like and unlike home. The rumbling of trucks at the rest stop is unlike home, which is symbolized by the peaceful image of the coffee in the pale cup on a wooden table. However, the scent of sage and wildflower at the rest stop is reminiscent of the natural feeling evoked by the coffee cup on the wooden table.

Urge students to incorporate a detail that captures the essence of the speaker's home. The detail should function as the key to the poem by providing a glimpse of the speaker's feelings about home. Students may wish to incorporate words or phrases from a language other than standard English (as Lance Henson does) to help evoke the atmosphere of the place.

PREWRITING

Have students generate a list of details (not necessarily positive ones) that capture the essence of home in the speaker's mind. Images may reflect the speaker's city, town, or region, or the actual family home.

Students should share their favorite details with the entire class. The class as a whole should suggest two or three more details that each student can add to his or her list.

PREWRITING SAMPLES

Details describing Los Angeles may include:

- *talking on a car phone in gridlock*

- *depot for buses to Mexico with huge luxury apartments in the background*

- *palms swaying against a dry, concrete riverbed filled with garbage*

- *light purple mountains glowing in the clear dawn*

Details that describe an individual's family home may include:

- *lace*

- *walls of photos*

- *baseball pennants and trophies*

- *a collection of antique boxes*

- *familiar drinking glasses*

- *the scent of garlic cooking*

LESSON 3
GUIDE: UPDATE OF "GIRL" BY JAMAICA KINCAID

In this lesson students will write a present-day guide for a young woman or man who is being taught by the family and community to be respectable and knowledgeable. The guide should include information and advice about what to do and what to watch out for regarding house-keeping, health, relationships, clothing, school, and jobs, and so on.

Ask students to reflect as closely as possible the cultural and family background of the young woman or man to whom they are writing. For instance, is he or she from a rural area or a city? Have students work individually or in groups to write a guide for a young person whose background is familiar to them or, using reference materials, for someone who is from a culture unfamiliar to them.

LESSON 4

POEM: AN ANCESTRAL PERSPECTIVE

based on "The Poet Imagines His Grandfather's Thoughts on the Day He Died"

The poet believes that his grandfather thought or hoped that some day one of his young grandchildren would think of him and imagine what he had seen. Under that assumption, the poem makes the grandfather's wish come true. In this lesson students will write a poem in which they imagine what one of their ancestors thought and perceived when he or she was a young man or woman.

PREWRITING

To start, have students find out as much as they can about one of their grandparents or great-grandparents. Suggest they gather information from interviews with relatives and from old photos that will help them imagine what their ancestor saw during a typical day when he or she was a young adult. Pose the following prompts to help students begin:

- *What did your ancestor's street, yard, garden, and means of transportation look like?*

- *How did he or she get around?*

- *What activities did he or she engage in around the house?*

- *What kind of work did your ancestor do?*

- *With what kind of clothes was your ancestor familiar?*

- *What languages did he or she speak?*

Suggest to students they use words from a language other than English to help depict the life of their ancestor. For instance, if a grandfather or great-grandfather was from Vietnam, they might wish to use some Vietnamese phrases in their poems.

In addition to these external aspects of life, urge students to find out about some of their ancestor's specific loves, fears, disappointments, and joys as a young adult. Challenge them to find out about some specific incidents that caused him or her to feel these emotions.

Lum's poem is composed of what he imagines to have been the thoughts of his grandfather. Tell students when they write their poems not to write in their own voices about what they see, but to write in their ancestor's voice about what they imagine he or she saw or felt.

Suggest that students end their poems, as Lum does, with the following or similar lines: "Maybe someday one of them will think of me/and see the _____ that I have seen"

Note: Encourage students to go back to a generation with which they are unfamiliar. For Wing Tek Lum, this was the generation of his grandfather; many students will probably have to go back further.

Create a special atmosphere for the class when they share their poems. You may want to serve tea and cookies or other refreshments.

LESSON 5
TRIBUTE SPEECH IN PERSONAL LIFE

Gail Harter, when she taught in Fillmore, California, developed a unit on tribute speeches. The following lesson is an adaptation. Family members may present their share of troubles, but they also can provide particular forms of support and valuable lessons. In this lesson students will write and prepare a tribute speech about a member of their immediate or extended family as if they were going to present it to a large family gathering in his or her honor. Students' speeches should be three to five minutes long and should be devoted to two or three major characteristics of the family member. Remind students to provide ample details that will bring the subject to life and please him or her.

PREWRITING

I. The following prompts are suggestions to help students generate their own ideas. They are not intended to be a format for students to model. Read the following prompts to students, giving them time to write the questions in their journals:

- *Why is this family member important to you?*

- *Is this person very helpful and kind to you? How?*

- *Does he or she sacrifice to help you survive or be happy? In what way?*

- *What does this person consciously and by their example teach you about life ?*

- *What attitudes about life does he or she hold that you like? For instance, is humor an important part of this person's life?*

- *Does he or she possess a kind of toughness? Does he or she set high goals and achieve them?*

- *Does this person have any special talents? For instance, is he or she an excellent story-teller, gardener, cook, or mechanic? Does he or she love languages?*

- *Does this person try to teach you the value of education? Explain.*

2. Instruct students to look over their responses to the prompts, and to jot down facts or episodes that demonstrate the particular qualities of the family member.

Have students share some of their favorite incidents with the class.

WRITING THE SPEECH

When students write their speeches, instruct them on the importance of carefully regarding the family member on his or her own terms, rather than examining how he or she fits externally prescribed molds. For example, the challenges facing parents are acknowledged in the poem "Ancestor" (*Hear My Voice*, page 141), in which the speaker is able to see what valuable gifts his imperfect father has given him.

Have students practice and then present their speeches in a small group or to the class. Whether they have memorized their speeches or are reading them, remind students to look at their audience often and to speak in a clear and confident voice.

This lesson works well as a speech, but you may wish to assign it as a written tribute in addition to or instead of the speech. You may wish to distribute scoring guidelines like the following to the class before they practice their speeches in small groups.

- *speaks in a voice that can be easily heard*

- *provides eye contact with the audience*

- *focuses on two or three positive qualities*

- *includes facts and incidents that demonstrate the admirable qualities of the subject*

Suggest students use the following numbers to rate each quality when their classmates make their final presentations:

1— needs improvement

2— satisfactory

3— excellent

This would be an excellent opportunity to invite parents to class or to an evening tribute "dessert" at which students present their speeches.

LESSON 6
TRIBUTE SPEECH IN LITERATURE

SUGGESTED WORKS FROM *HEAR MY VOICE*
"Mommy, What Does 'Nigger' Mean?" page 45
In Search of Our Mothers' Gardens, page 127
Ancestor, page 141
Those Winter Sundays, page 143
I Stand Here Ironing, page 158
In the American Society, page 174
My Mother's Stories, page 189
The Lesson, page 216
Each Year Grain, page 252
My Dungeon Shook: Letter to My Nephew on the One Hundredth
    Anniversary of the Emancipation, page 277
The Woman Who Makes Swell Doughnuts, page 367

SUGGESTED LONGER WORKS:
Out of this Furnace, Thomas Bell
A Yellow Raft in Blue Water, Michael Dorris
Love Medicine, Louise Erdrich
Tracks, Louise Erdrich
Tell Me a Riddle, Tillie Olsen
Clover, Dori Sanders
King Lear, William Shakespeare
The Joy Luck Club, Amy Tan

The Kitchen God's Wife, Amy Tan

Memory of Kin: Stories About Family by Black Writers, edited by Mary Helen Washington

Homebase, Shawn Wong

In this lesson students will write and prepare a speech of tribute that a character from one of the selections listed above might make at a family gathering about a family member . Suggest that students focus on two or three general characteristics that are admirable or positive and on specific supporting details as well. Instruct students to use details from the work of literature and to create examples that could be true of the character but are not actually in the work.

PREWRITING

1. Use the same prompts that are suggested in Lesson 5, Tribute Speech in Personal Life, page 39.

2. Have students refer to the literature they are reading to find details for their speech.

3. Go around the room and have students read aloud parts of the work they will use for supporting details.

You may wish to have students present their tribute speeches to small groups or to the entire class. Use the scoring guidelines provided on pages 40 and 41.

This lesson works especially well when students (or groups of students) are reading different works.

LESSON 7

LITERATURE JOURNAL: HOW FAMILIES INFLUENCE DEVELOPMENT

WRITING ABOUT LITERATURE

Have students write about characters from two or more works in this anthology and discuss, using examples, the positive and negative influences they received from their families. Ask students to predict what the future might bring for the characters because of the way they were raised and to provide justification for their predictions.

PERSONAL WRITING

Have students write about themselves and their families. Ask them to consider how their family influences them and what will be the effects of their upbringing in their future.

You may wish to ask students to share and discuss their journal entries in small groups. Tell students that this is not a critical exercise and they should not attempt to judge or correct other students' entries. Urge students instead to listen closely as each student reads his or her journal entry and to make specific, nonjudgmental comments about the entry.

LESSON 8
A SIGNIFICANT ADULT WRITES TO A YOUNGER PERSON

Jackie Ellenz, of Portland, Oregon, developed a unit that begins with the reading of "A Christmas Memory" by Truman Capote, and ends with an extensive version of Variation B of this lesson. What follows here is an adaptation of her unit.

SUGGESTED WORKS FROM *HEAR MY VOICE*
I'll Crack Your Head Kotsun, page 34
"Mommy, What Does 'Nigger' Mean?" page 45
In Search of Our Mothers' Gardens, page 127
Ancestor, page 141
Those Winter Sundays, page 143
The Bending of a Twig, page 145
I Stand Here Ironing, page 158
In the American Society, page 174
Girl, page 200

VARIATIONS

A. Much of the literature in this anthology is about the relationships between young people and the adults who are very important to them. Have students choose one of the works listed above and write a letter to the younger person from a significant adult. Instruct them to write the letter as if a number of years had gone by since the time of the story or poem and to make clear within the letter when and why it is being written. The occasion of the letter may be a death in the family, a birth, graduation, marriage, birthday, an imprisonment, or traditional gathering. Remind students to be certain the letter has a focus: Does the older family member advise, apologize, inquire, inspire?

B. Have students write a letter to themselves from a significant adult in their life.

PREWRITING PROMPTS

- *Form a list of significant people in your life, and choose one person about whom to write. Begin with "I am thankful for_____" and write for ten minutes without stopping.*

Go around the room and have each student share a small portion of what he or she wrote.

- *Think about details that characterize this significant person. Write without stopping for ten minutes.*

Again, have each student share a favorite part of their writing.

- *Switch points of view and write in the voice of the adult about whom you have been thinking. What does this person think and feel about significant aspects of his or her life? You may want to include how they feel about their family, friends, and work, as well as their priorities, values, and goals. After ten minutes, share a part with the class.*

- *Write a letter from this person to you. As in Variation A., make clear within the letter when and why it is being written. How does he or she see you and your life? How does this person see your relationship now and in the past? What would he or she want to say to you? (You may want to use some parts of what you have already written about this person.)*

LESSON 9
LITERATURE JOURNAL: JOYS AND DISAPPOINTMENTS OF FAMILY LIFE

SUGGGESTED WORKS FROM *HEAR MY VOICE*
"Mommy, What Does 'Nigger' Mean?" page 45
She Is Beautiful in Her Whole Being, page 94
Anniversary, page 115
In Search of Our Mothers' Gardens, page 127
A Moving Day, page 135
Ancestor, page 141

The Bending of a Twig, page 145
Scribbles, page 153
I Stand Here Ironing, page 158
From *A Bintel Brief:* Letters from the World of Our Fathers, page 169
My Mother's Stories, page 189
Girl, page 200

SUGGESTED LONGER WORKS
see Family and Generations, Lesson 1, page 35, and Lesson 6, page 41

Ask students to reflect in their literature journals on how family relations (between children and parents, between parents, and between members of an extended family) can be an important source of fulfillment and sustenance for an individual on the one hand, or a significant source of disappointment and pain on the other. Have students choose at least three works in the *Hear My Voice* anthology to discuss, and instruct them to use details from the works to justify their points. Ask students to explain, if possible, why they chose these particular works.

LESSON 10
LITERATURE JOURNAL/DISCUSSION: COMPARE FAMILIES YOU KNOW TO FAMILIES IN LITERATURE AND ON TELEVISION

1. Ask students which television families they find most like their own family and those around them and which television families are the least real to them. Have students explain their responses fully. Aspects of television families they may wish to consider include:

- *Socioeconomic factors: How closely do television families match your own? Compare the types of jobs people have. Who works? How much leisure time do the characters have? How does this compare to the leisure time in your home?*

- *If school life is portrayed, how similar is it to yours?*

- *Do members of the television families do the same kind of things when they are not at work or school as do your family members?*

- *How similar are speech patterns, word choices, and dialects in real and television families?*

- *Are gender roles in real and television families alike?*

- *Are conflicts the result of similar root causes in real and television families and are they resolved in a similar fashion?*

2. Ask students which families in the selections of this anthology are the most like their own family and those families close to them and which are least real to them. Have students explain their responses fully.

3. Have each member of the class rank the stories about relationships within families (using the suggested works from *Hear My Voice* from Lesson 9, Family and Generations, page 44) as to how well they could be adapted to a new television series.

4. Organize a class discussion to complete the following statement:

The three stories best suited to be the basis of a provocative new television series are _____, _____, and _____. Challenge the class to support their choices and develop a consensus.

LESSON 11

TELLING FAMILY STORIES
based on "My Mother's Stories" by Tony Ardizzone

Family members love to tell and embellish humorous, sad, and thought-provoking stories about the family's cast of characters. In this lesson students will write their favorite stories about their own family members.

PREWRITING—RESEARCH AND NOTE-TAKING

Direct students to ask a number of relatives to tell them as much as they can remember of the stories that get told and retold in their families. Suggest they ask to hear stories about what adults were like when they were young and about how couples met, fell in love, and married.

- *Who in the family was particularly brave?*

- *Did anyone have brushes with supernatural events?*

- *Are there any interesting stories about accidents?*

- *Are there any humorous stories?*

- *Are there any army or war stories?*

- *Were there any exciting escapes?*

Remind students to be sure to interview older members of the family and to ask more than one person about the same story in order to gain a broader and more accurate perspective.

WRITING AND PUBLISHING

Have students choose one story about which to write. Suggest to students they try to capture the oral quality of the stories by building suspense and using dialogue.

The compilation of these stories makes a wonderful class magazine. Whether or not the class publishes a magazine, the students can tell their stories at a family night in which parents may further embellish the stories, as well as tell new ones.

LESSON 12

FAMILY TREES IN A WORK OF LITERATURE

SUGGESTED LONGER WORKS

Bless Me, Ultima, Rudolfo Anaya

Umbertina, Helen Barolini

Love Medicine, Louise Erdrich

Tracks, Louise Erdrich

The Forsyte Saga, John Galsworthy

Roots, Alex Haley

Migrant Souls, Arturo Islas

Winterkill, Craig Leslie

Riversong, Craig Leslie

One Hundred Years of Solitude, Gabriel García Marquez

Mama Day, Gloria Naylor

The Joy Luck Club, Amy Tan

FAMILY TREE

Have students draw as complete a family tree as possible for one of the works listed above, indicating marriages, parents, children, siblings, uncles, aunts, cousins, and so on. (See the family tree diagram in Lesson 13, page 49.) As much as possible, include physical characteristics, personality traits, and problems facing each of the main characters. Discuss with students the idea that issues facing a character usually derive from problems in the natural world, conflicts with other people, or conflicts internal to the character himself. Have students write all information in small letters on the tree next to each character's name.

Have students reflect in their journals on the completed family trees and the process of compiling the information.

- *Do the details in the tree help you understand why the characters behave with one another as they do?*

- *Can you see connections you did not previously see between characters?*

- *Can you identify any patterns? If so, what are they?*

LESSON 13
PERSONAL USE OF FAMILY TREES

This is a very delicate assignment. In certain cases it cannot be done without a tremendous amount of trust since a student's family life can be painful or embarrassing to reveal. On the other hand, it offers students a chance to view their family drama with a more objective eye.

FAMILY TREE

Ask students to construct their own family trees indicating marriages, parents, siblings, uncles, aunts, cousins, and so on. Have students conduct personal interviews with as many of their relatives as possible to obtain important dates, physical and personality characteristics, and the main problems facing the members of their families.

JOURNAL ENTRY

Have students reflect in their journals on the completed family trees and the process of compiling the information.

- *Do the details in the tree help you understand why family members behave with one another as they do?*

- *Do the details in the tree give you new perspectives on particular family members?*

- *Can you identify any patterns? If so, what are they?*

Note: If Ann Smith were doing her genealogy, she would construct a tree for her mother's family and her father's family. This tree traces Ann's mother's family. Also note I have used two different shapes to indicate male and female family members and crossed lines to indicate separations.

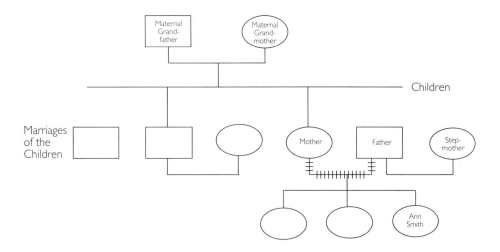

LESSON 14

COLLAGE REPRESENTING A FAMILY MEMBER

Tell students that they will create a collage representing a family member. Guide students to use visual materials that portray this person's passions (painting cars, fighting racism, building boats, dancing), quirks, favorites (foods, music, sports, places), problems, values, skills, experiences, favorite people, etc.

Students' collages can be quite elaborate. Some students may wish to construct their collages using many kinds of materials and objects sewn onto a cloth backing. Other students may find collages composed of photos and magazine pictures mounted on paper a more effective medium to communicate their messages.

Suggest drawings, magazine pictures, photographs, ribbons, clothing, diplomas, tickets, and objects representing hobbies or jobs, such as guitar strings, knitting yarn, and other mementos as possible collage materials.

The class may wish to arrange their individual collages in a formal quilt design after studying traditional American quilt patterns, or they may wish to create a free-form quilt design. If the class aims to create a specific quilt pattern, students should construct individual collages on paper or cloth of a variety of shapes.

The class, a group of classes, or the entire school might put together an exhibition of collages as a visual tribute to the families of the students.

You may want to host a community celebration to unveil the collages.

LESSON 15
BIOGRAPHICAL ESSAY ABOUT A FAMILY MEMBER

In this essay, have students use incidents, descriptions, and dialogue to convey to readers the particular personality of a member of their family. Tell students that although the major focus of this essay is the family member, the secondary focus is their relation to this person. Suggest they select details carefully so the tone of the essay will reflect love, admiration, anger, or whichever emotion accurately expresses their feelings when they contemplate this person.

PREWRITING

- *Memory writing: Write notes on significant incidents involving the family member about whom you are writing. What incidents do you remember observing?*

- *Interview other family members to find out their perspectives about your subject. Ask them what kind of person they feel the subject is and how their own lives have been affected by the subject. What events and conversations do they remember? Ask other family members to tell you any family stories about your subject. (See Lesson 11 on family stories).*

- *Construct a collage representing the person you are writing about (Lesson 14).*

LESSON 16
AUTOBIOGRAPHICAL INCIDENT INVOLVING A FAMILY MEMBER

In this essay, the relative importance of the topics in the biographical essay is different: the person writing receives the major treatment and a family member receives the secondary focus. For this autobiographical essay, have students present and analyze a significant event in their lives in which they and a family member interacted.

PREWRITING

Ask students to list incidents involving other family members and themselves that they feel were somehow significant. Students may wish to proceed chronologically or they may wish to remember incidents randomly. Once students have completed the lists, instruct them to jot next to each event its personal significance. Have students choose their essay topics from this list.

WRITING THE FIRST DRAFT

The incident students describe may be an ordinary occurrence or an unusual event. Provide the following examples for students:

- *your mom taught you to ride a bike*

- *you went fishing with your brother in the early morning*

- *your father carried you home from the hospital after an operation*

- *your older cousin took you to a major league baseball game*

- *you stayed home from a date to take care of your sick sister*

Remind students to provide ample details describing the scene and people present and to tell what happened, using dialogue if appropriate.

Have students present sufficient background information about themselves and significant details about the event to emphasize the significance of the incident for them. For example, a student may show how work took so much of her mother's time that she saw her infrequently. The essay may go on to show how much it meant to her that her mother was at the hospital with comic books when her tonsils were taken out.

LESSON 17
DEBATE ON TRADITIONS: IRRELEVANT VOICES FROM THE PAST OR GUIDES FOR THE PRESENT?

PRE-DEBATE JOURNAL WRITING

Have students jot their responses to the following:

- *What are some traditions in your family or community? Do you eat particular traditional foods, attend holiday celebrations and festivals, participate in religious ceremonies, or conduct rituals around birth, special birthdays, coming of age, marriage, anniversaries, and death? Are these traditions of your ethnic group or of your particular family? (Often individual families have their own ways of honoring ethnic or national customs.)*

- *Who, if anyone, is the main person upholding the traditions in your extended family?*

- *How useful or enjoyable do you find these traditions? Are there any traditions you think might be harmful in some way? Explain.*

DEBATE

All students should take a stand on the discussion topic: "Traditions are just voices from the past and are no longer needed today."

There are many formats for debates. One format that I use is simply to have everyone in the class speak on the issue. I call on students in the order they raise their hands. They can introduce new ideas, agree or disagree with someone, or support one of the stated positions. They get extra credit when they mention some of the other speakers by name and can remember those speakers' positions.

LESSON 18
JOURNAL ENTRY/DISCUSSION: RENEWING AND CREATING TRADITIONS

In small groups or pairs, have students create "new" traditions for their community. Many people have lost touch with a number of family and community traditions and have not replaced them with anything new. Ask students:

- *If you could create some traditions, what would they be like?*

- *What holidays would you celebrate? Why?*

- *Are there some special historical events or people you would like to commemorate?*

- *Would you celebrate new holidays? Which ones? Explain.*

- *Would you create rituals marking passages like birth, birthdays, various graduations, becoming an adult, marriage, death, and seasons? Would you create rituals showing respect for nature or some part of it?*

- *Describe the ceremonies or festivities in detail.*

Have students share ideas from their small groups with the entire class. Create a class chart of new and renewed traditions.

SOCIETY: CONFLICT, STRUGGLE, AND CHANGE

*P*EOPLE OFTEN FEEL ALIENATED from what they read in the newspaper or hear on television and radio news. They wonder, "What do politics, economics, and statistics have to do with me?" One of the best ways to understand the importance of history and current events is to examine social issues as they affect individuals. Literature, like drama, film, visual art, and music, can transform social and political issues into something personal and vital.

LESSON I
SPEECH: DREAMS FOR SOCIETY
based on "I Have A Dream" by Dr. Martin Luther King, Jr.

PREWRITING

1. Conduct a class oral reading of "I Have a Dream," asking individual students to take turns reading sections of the speech. If possible, play a recording of King giving the speech.

2. In a class discussion analyze the structure of the last part of the speech, starting with "So I say to you, my friends, that even though we must face the difficulties of today and tomorrow, I still have a dream...."

- *Where does Dr. King repeat, "I have a dream"?*

- *What general truths or exclamations does he express? An example of an exclamation is "Let freedom ring."*

- *What specific dreams does King express? An example of a specific dream is, "I have a dream that one day, down in Alabama, with its vicious racists, with its governor having his lips dripping with the words of interposition and nullification, that one day right there in Alabama, little black boys and black girls will be able to join hands with little white boys and white girls as sisters and brothers."*

3. Ask individuals or small groups to brainstorm a list of present day dreams they have for society. Some possibilities may include that people not be judged by:

- *the color of their skin*

- *how much money they make*

- *how fashionable they are*

- *how popular they are*

- *their age*

Students may also want to address such issues as the treatment of women, Native Americans, African Americans, teenagers, the environment, cruelty to animals, unequal distribution of wealth, or war.

WRITING THE DRAFT

4. Instruct students to write their own "I Have A Dream" speeches in which they focus on a single injustice or address a series of injustices. Have students provide specific instances of the injustice and also paint a detailed picture of the ideal they envision, using repetition to emphasize key phrases. Tell students to feel free to use as many as they wish of King's actual words or words from other famous speeches, songs, and documents.

SAMPLE OF THE BEGINNING OF A SPEECH MODELED ON "I HAVE A DREAM"

We hold these truths to be self-evident, that all people are endowed by their creator with certain inalienable rights, that among these are Life, Liberty, and the pursuit of Happiness. I have a dream that one day in the cities and towns of this country, all children will be able to pursue happiness and follow their star. I have a dream that one day the more than 40 percent of New York's children who live below the poverty line will never have to deal with rats in their beds and drug dealers in their hallways, but instead will be free to turn their attention more fully to learning about this universe.

My dream today is that proclamations about "The Year Of The Child" will be made real at the bottom line and that for all children this will be the sweet land of opportunity.

DELIVERING THE SPEECH

5. Have students practice delivering their speeches in front of a mirror or with a videocamera. Suggest they further revise their speeches as they

practice. Encourage students to vary the volume and tempo and to use silence to create drama and intensity. Have students present their speeches to the class.

LESSON 2
LITERATURE JOURNAL/SKITWRITING: DIALOGUE BETWEEN MARTIN LUTHER KING, JR., AND OTHERS ON STRATEGIES FOR DEALING WITH INJUSTICE

SUGGESTED WORKS FROM *HEAR MY VOICE*
Wasichus in the Hills, page 205
Concentration Constellation, page 213
The Lesson, page 216
Each Year Grain, page 252
They Say Them Child Brides Don't Last, page 257
Tony's Story, page 265

SUGGESTED LONGER WORKS
*Making Waves, edited by Asian Women United of California
*Out of This Furnace, Thomas Bell
*Bury My Heart at Wounded Knee, Dee Brown
*Lakota Woman, Mary Crow Dog
*The Autobiography of Malcolm X, as told to Alex Haley
Justice Delayed: The Record of the Japanese-American Internment Cases, Peter Irons
*Malcolm X Speaks: Selected Speeches and Statements, Malcolm X
*In the Spirit of Crazy Horse, Peter Matthiessen
*Black Elk Speaks, as told to John G. Neihardt
The Grapes of Wrath, John Steinbeck

Ask students to imagine that characters or individuals from some of the fiction and nonfiction works listed above and Martin Luther King, Jr., are seated at a table discussing their personal struggles against injustices. Students may wish to include characters from the *Hear My Voice* anthology and from longer works that they are studying. Ask students to use what they know of King's views from "I Have a Dream" and "Letter From a Birmingham Jail" to imagine what advice and criticism he might give to the people who are seated at the table. Ask students how the characters might respond, what issues might be raised, and what their opinions are on these issues.

You may have students write about these issues in their journals, and then in pairs or groups script a scene in which the various characters converse about their experiences with injustice and thier strategies for social change. Students may then present their scenes to the class.

LESSON 3

POEMS: CINQUAINS ABOUT THE AMERICAS
based on "This Is the Land" by Carlos Cortez

A spatial sweep of the hemisphere as well as a sweep over time provides the setting for this bilingual poem about the migrations of people across the Americas. Cortez eerily portrays the lives of many generations on the same land almost simultaneously. Cortez' panoramic view places the issue of justice at the border in a clear perspective.

PREWRITING

1. In groups, pairs, or as a class, have students identify and research the time frame of all the migrations described in the poem. Ask students to trace these migrations on a map of the Western Hemisphere. Students will probably need to use library reference materials in their research.

2. Again in groups, pairs, or as a class, have students brainstorm two lists of phrases and images from Cortez' poem. The first list should be about the time before the "invader," and the second about the time since the "invader." Items on the first list might include llanos, tribesmen, buffalo, the Arapaho, the Kansa, La Raza, and Tenochtitlan. Items on the second list might include motorists, semidrivers, homesteaders, Okies, los alambres, and Disneyland.

WRITING THE DRAFT

3. Students will write two cinquains, one about the time before the invader and one about the time since. For the first poem, direct them to choose an image or word from "This Is the Land" about the Great Plains before the invader for the first line of the cinquain and, in the remainder of the poem, to use their own ideas as well as Cortez'. Then have them write a cinquain based on a modern image of the Great Plains from "This Is the Land." Instruct them to use this word or

image for the first line of the second cinquain and, again, any combination of their own thoughts and Cortez'.

Students may choose to make their poems bilingual.

ILLUSTRATING THE POEMS

4. Have students draw pictures or use photos from magazines to illustrate their poems.

Note: If students are unfamiliar with the form of a cinquain, you may wish to explain that a cinquain is a five-line poem. The first line contains one word that names the poem's subject. The second line contains two words that describe the subject. The third line contains three words that express an action associated with the subject. The fourth line contains four words that express a personal attitude towards the subject. The fifth line has one word that summarizes, restates, or supplies a synonym for the subject.

SAMPLE CINQUAIN

Mojados[1]
van norte[2]
Cross their river
Fugitives in *their* land
Indios[3]

LESSON 4

FILM CRITIQUE/EXTENDED JOURNAL WRITING: POINT OF VIEW INFLUENCES HOW ETHNIC AND CULTURAL GROUPS ARE PORTRAYED

This project involves comparing portrayals of ethnic and cultural groups as they are found in a variety of films. The purpose of this lesson is to develop critical thinking skills regarding point of view and to demonstrate the need for using a wide variety of sources in order to understand another's point of view and establish one's own point of view.

---

1.   Mojados—The wetbacks (derogatory term)
2.   van norte—they go north
3.   Indios—Indians

Make some of the films listed below available for students to view in small groups or as a class. You may wish to preview the films and assign students to view certain scenes or you may wish to have students watch one or more films in their entirety. Some of the films listed below are produced by people of the cultural or ethnic group that the film portrays, others are not. I suggest you always preview a film to assure its appropriateness. You may wish to omit certain portions or to obtain parental permission for some videos. In addition, it may be important to check with your supervisors about policy for viewing copywritten material in school.

Before students view the films, explain that some of them contain authentic portrayals that would be acceptable to many members of the cultural group, while others include stereotypical images. In some movies, members of certain cultural groups may be portrayed as ruthless, savage, crazed, or primitive. Other portrayals that seem kinder, but which nevertheless impart a false view, may include portrayals of people from particular cultural groups as passive, dull, nonverbal, or humorless. Some movies make a point of creating "ideal" members of a particular group, thus highlighting the "bad" ones. Try to help students recognize the danger and power of such biased filmmaking.

FILMS BY AND ABOUT NATIVE AMERICANS
Cheyenne Autumn
Dances With Wolves
Drums Along The Mohawk
Fort Apache
†*Incident at Oglala* (Facets Video, 1517 West Fullerton Avenue, Chicago, IL 60614, (800) 331-6197))
†*Itam Makim Hopiit* (Facets Video, 1517 West Fullerton Avenue, Chicago, IL 60614, (800) 331-6197)
Little Big Man
Rio Grande
She Wore A Yellow Ribbon
Stagecoach
The Searchers
The Last of the Mohicans

FILMS BY AND ABOUT AFRICAN AMERICANS
Attack on Terror (a dramatization of the murder of three civil rights workers, addressing the same topic as *Mississippi Burning*)

Boyz 'N the Hood
Driving Miss Daisy
Gone With The Wind
Glory
Guess Who's Coming to Dinner
†*Hollywood Shuffle* (M.C.E.G./Sterling, 2121 Avenue of the Stars, Suite 2630, Los Angeles, CA 90067, (310) 282-0871)
Huckleberry Finn
Malcolm X
Mississippi Burning
†*The Brother from Another Planet* (Facets Video, 1517 West Fullerton Avenue, Chicago, IL 60614, (800) 331-6197)
To Kill A Mockingbird
To Sleep With Anger

FILMS BY AND ABOUT ASIAN AMERICANS
†*A Great Wall* (Pacific Arts Video, #6300219658, 11858 La Grange Avenue, Los Angeles, CA 90025, (800) 282-8765)
†*Alamo Bay* (RCA/Columbia Home Video #6300139174, Columbia/Tristar Home Video, 3400 Riverside Drive, Burbank, CA 91505, (818) 972-8193)
†*Chan Is Missing* (New Yorker Films Video, #6301551664, 16 West 61st Street, New York, NY 10023, (800) 447-0196)
Charlie Chan movies
†*Come See the Paradise* (CBS/Fox Video #6302041147)
†*Dim Sum: A Little Bit of Heart,* subtitled (Pacific Arts Video, #630021, 11858 La Grange Avenue, Los Angeles, CA 90025, (800) 282-8765)
†*Eat a Bowl of Tea* (RCA/Columbia Home Video, Columbia/Tristar Home Video, #6301574591, Columbia Tristar Home Video, 3400 Riverside Drive, Burbank, CA 91505, (818) 972-8193)
Flower Drum Song
Sixteen Candles
Teahouse of the August Moon

FILMS BY AND ABOUT LATINOS
El Norte (contains some strong language)
Fort Apache, The Bronx
La Bamba
†*Salt of the Earth* (NPI Home Video, #1360, 15825 Rob Roy Drive, Oak Forest, IL 60452, (800) 322-0442)

Stand and Deliver

The Border

The Milagro Beanfield War

†*Zoot Suit* (MCA/Universal Home Video, Inc., 70 Universal City Plaza, Suite 435, Los Angeles, CA 91608, (818) 777-5539)

FILMS BY AND ABOUT ITALIAN AMERICANS

†*Dominic and Eugene* (Facets Video, 1517 West Fullerton Avenue, Chicago, IL 60614, (800) 331-6197)

Marty

Moonstruck

Rocky

The Freshman

The Godfather

The Wanderers

FILMS BY AND ABOUT JEWISH AMERICANS

Delancy Street

†*Tell Me a Riddle* (Media Home Entertainment/Heron Communications, 510 West 6th Street, Suite 1032, Los Angeles, CA 90014, (213) 236-1336)

†*The Killing Floor* (depicts African-American, Polish, Lithuanian, Irish, and German slaughterhouse workers in Chicago during World War I), (Columbia/Tristar Home Video, 3400 Riverside Drive, Burbank, CA 91505, (818) 972-8193)

FILMS BY AND ABOUT ARAB AMERICANS

Aladdin

Black Sunday (includes violence)

†*The Suitors* (Facets Video, 1517 West Fullerton Avenue, Chicago, IL 60614, (800) 331-6197)

† These movies can be found at video rental shops that include works by independent filmmakers. You can also contact the distributors directly. Other films listed are available at most video rental shops.

Distribute and discuss the questions on page 62 before students view a film, but ask them to fill in their responses after watching the film. Remind students to provide specific examples from the movie to support their responses. They may need to view sections of a film more than once.

Viewing and critiquing films provides a good opportunity to compare how filmmakers portray historical events and periods to depictions in other sources. You may wish to make available to students works of fiction and nonfiction, especially for question 8 on the worksheet. I suggest using the *Hear My Voice Bibliography* for ideas for materials.

Encourage students who have viewed the same film to discuss their responses. You may want to encourage "teams" of students to view a few films as a group and compare their responses to the various films.

VARIATION

Have students read one or more of the works listed below. Then ask them to respond to the questions on the film critique worksheet, adapting the questions to fit a literary work rather than a film. Students may gain a clearer perspective on literary and film techniques by having to shift the terminology.

SUGGESTED WORKS FROM *HEAR MY VOICE*
Notes from a Fragmented Daughter, page 23
"Mommy, What Does 'Nigger' Mean?" page 45
A Seat in the Garden, page 50
Juke Box Love Song, page 81
She Is Beautiful in Her Whole Being, page 94
A Certain Beginning, page 101
Anniversary, page 115
Finding a Wife, page 117
In Search of Our Mothers' Gardens, page 127
Those Winter Sundays, page 143
Wasichus in the Hills, page 205
The Lesson, page 216
Each Year Grain, page 252
Tony's Story, page 265
From *Donald Duk*, page 292
Flying Home, page 298

FILM CRITIQUE

Respond to the following questions on a separate piece of paper.

1. Did you like the film? Why or why not?

Carefully note the characters' tones of voice, facial expressions, and body language in order to answer questions 2 and 3.

2. Describe how the characters relate to one another in the movie. What feelings, attitudes, and thoughts do they express? What is the range of human emotions expressed by the characters? Are the characters portrayed as being intelligent, wise, or thoughtful? Which characters have major speaking parts? Do you feel any characters are portrayed in a stereotypical manner? If so, which ones? In what ways?

3. What conflicts occur in the film? When a conflict occurs, are both sides portrayed fairly and realistically, or is the point of view of one side given more emphasis than the other?

4. Describe the filmmaker's techniques. For instance, how does the filmmaker use closeups? Does the filmmaker use different angles for different characters? Are different lighting styles used for certain characters and scenes? How is music used? How do these and other techniques affect your response to characters and scenes?

5. Is there a hero or heroine? Which characters do you feel you know best? Which character or characters do you "root" for? With which characters do you most closely identify? How much of your response to the characters is based on the filmmaker's techniques and how much is based on your personal predilections?

6. What is the climax or turning point of the story?

7. Who do you think created this film? Did the film receive a wide distribution? Were people from the cultural groups portrayed involved in writing, directing, and acting in the film? When was this film made? Why was this film made? Is there a message?

8. What is the setting of the film? Is it a setting with which you are familiar? Does the film accurately portray such a setting? What world and national events and trends might the writers and filmmakers have been emphasizing, omitting, or obscuring? Use your history textbook and other sources to supplement your own knowledge.

9. Using your responses to questions 1–8, consider from whose point of view the story in the film is told.

SUGGESTED LONGER WORKS

The Dream Book: An Anthology of Writings by Italian-American Women, edited by
    Helen Barolini

**Bury My Heart at Wounded Knee*, Dee Brown

**The Last of the Menu Girls*, Denise Chavez

**Donald Duk*, Frank Chin

**Eat a Bowl of Tea*, Louis Chu

**Yellow Raft in Blue Water*, Michael Dorris

**Love Medicine*, Louise Erdrich

**Through and Through: Toledo Stories*, Joseph Geha

**Jews Without Money*, Michael Gold

**The Floating World*, Cynthia Kadohata

**Medicine River*, Thomas King

**China Boy*, Gus Lee

To Kill a Mockingbird, Harper Lee

**Riversong*, Craig Leslie

**Winterkill*, Craig Leslie

**The Forbidden Stitch: An Asian-American Women's Anthology*, edited by Shirley
    Geok-Lin Lim and Mayumi Tsutakawa

**Yokohama, California*, Toshio Mori

**Black Elk Speaks*, as told to John G. Neihardt

George Washington Gómez, Américo Paredes

Trini, Estela Portillo Trambley

**Y No Se lo Trago la Tierra/ And the Earth Did Not Devour Him*, Tomas Rivera

**Hunger of Memory*, Richard Rodriguez

**Ceremony*, Leslie Marmon Silko

**North of the Rio Grande: The Mexican-American Experience in Short Fiction*, edited
    by Edward Simmen

**Small Faces*, Gary Soto

**Puerto Rican Writers at Home in the U.S.A.*, edited by Faythe Turner

FURTHER VARIATIONS

A. Ask students to use the film critique worksheet in order to compare
two different works on the same general topic. For example, students
can respond to the movie "Cheyenne Autumn" as well as Chapter 14
of the book *Bury My Heart At Wounded Knee*, "Cheyenne Exodus," or the
book *Cheyenne Autumn* by Mari Sandoz. Similarly, students can respond
to the movie *Gone With the Wind* as well as *Jubilee*, a book about the Civil

War by Margaret Walker, or *Beloved*, a book about the aftermath of the Civil War by Toni Morrison.

B. As a class or in small groups, have students compare different portrayals of an ethnic or cultural group by creating a chart to summarize responses to Questions 2–8 for a number of movies and literary works.

LESSON 5
WRITE A LETTER TO MEDIA PRODUCERS AND CRITICS ABOUT THE REPRESENTATION OF VARIOUS CULTURAL GROUPS IN POPULAR FILMS

If your students found cultural representation lacking or inaccurate in the works they reviewed and in the previous lesson, this activity may help create something constructive out of their frustration or sense of injustice.

As individuals, in groups, or as a class, have students write letters to magazines, newspapers, and film companies expressing their reasoned opinions on the representation of different cultural groups in the popular media. They may wish to write to these people about their findings from Lesson 4. Other questions to consider include:

- *What would be some of the effects on life in the United States if more popular movies were produced from the points of view of America's diverse cultural groups? What are the effects of racist and stereotypical representations on members of different groups?*

- *Which movies and television representations of various cultures (if any) would you rate highly? Explain. Which movies and television representations (if any) do you feel portray a culture unjustly or unfairly? Explain.*

- *What kinds of characters would you want to see portrayed? Explain.*

- *What novels, plays, or short stories do you imagine would make good movies? Explain why these works would make good movies in terms of audience and purpose.*

LESSON 6
SHORT STORIES: A CONFLICT FROM TWO POINTS OF VIEW

1. In this lesson, students will write two short stories about a conflict, developing characters through description, narration, and dialogue. Ask them to write each story from the point of view of one of the parties involved in the conflict.

Instead of asking all students to write two stories, you may wish to have some students write a story from one point of view in a conflict and have the others write from a different point of view. You can divide the class into two parts with one half of the class writing from the point of view of one side of a conflict, and the other half writing from another side. Or you can have pairs of students choose a conflict and each write from a different point of view.

2. The two points of view from which students write may both be valid, or one or both viewpoints may obscure reality by omission, unfair selection, or falsification.

PREWRITING

3. Direct students to brainstorm possible situations involving conflict, explaining that some may come directly from their own experiences, while others may be situations they have observed or read about. Some suggestions of conflict areas include: teenagers and adults, friends or siblings, cliques in a school, ethnic groups, and employers and employees.

4. Ask students to jot down ideas about the main characters' personalities and the story line before they begin their drafts.

LESSON 7
POEM: TWO OPPOSING VOICES SPEAK ABOUT THE SAME SITUATION

In this lesson students will write a poem in which alternating lines express two individuals' conflicting points of view about the same situation. They may wish to describe a situation and develop the two first-person narratives so the reader will be sympathetic towards one of them and be critical of the other, or they may wish to create a situation in which the reader will be sympathetic to both voices.

IDEAS FOR CHARACTERS AND SETTINGS

* *Use the conflict from one of the stories in this section or a related work and write from the points of view of characters; for instance, Tony and the state cop in "Tony's Story" or Florence Reece's family and the coal company owners. Feel free to go beyond the plot.*

* *Borrow from literature: You can make up events, but use the setting and characters from one of the works in this anthology or related books. For instance, you may be inspired by Bury My Heart At Wounded Knee to write about a conflict between a Cheyenne and an official of the United States government. "The Lesson" may suggest a poem in the voices of Sylvia and the owner of F.A.O. Schwartz.*

- *Make up your own characters and settings: You may develop setting, characters, and events from your own experience and observations.*

Before they begin to write, have students brainstorm a list of possible situations and characters about which to write.

After students have drafted and edited their poems, have them practice reading the poems in two voices with partners before performing them for the class.

LESSON 8
ORAL LITERACY: GAINING DEEPER INSIGHT INTO CHARACTERS

I learned about the concepts of "hot seat" and "oral literacy" used in this lesson from Virginia Cotsis of Ventura, California.

SUGGESTED WORKS FROM *HEAR MY VOICE*
Wasichus in the Hills, page 205
The Lesson, page 216
Each Year Grain, page 252
They Say Them Child Brides Don't Last, page 257
Tony's Story, page 265
My Dungeon Shook, Letter to My Nephew on the One Hundredth
    Anniversary of the Emancipation, page 277
From *I Know Why the Caged Bird Sings*, page 286
From *Donald Duk*, page 292
Flying Home, page 298
Autumn Gardening, page 317
South Brooklyn, 1947, page 325
The English Lesson, page 377

SUGGESTED LONGER WORKS
This lesson may be used to help students understand virtually any novel.

The object of this lesson is to hear the voices of the characters in literature. This lesson is especially appropriate for understanding literature portraying people who are often invisible in society. Students will address at least five questions to selected major and minor characters in a story or essay. Everyone in the class will take turns being in the "hot seat." The person in the "hot seat" assumes the personality of the character being questioned and responds to other students' questions in keeping with the character's personality. Suggest to students in the "hot seat" that they examine the work closely and try to mimic the character's body language and tone of voice in various situations.

WRITING THE QUESTIONS

Students' goals in writing and asking these questions is to discover characters' motivations, values, and past experiences. Suggest that students think of themselves as investigative reporters as they write and ask questions. Encourage them to probe with thoughtful followup questions rather than settling for short answers. The questions may relate to the actual plot and they may also cover topics that could easily fit into the plot.

BEING IN THE "HOT SEAT"

Have students reread the work in which their character appears, paying particular attention to the character's body language, tone of voice, and reactions to other people. Urge students to try to stay in character at all times when responding to questions.

In order to ensure that all students have the opportunity to respond in a character's voice, you may want to conduct this activity in small groups with a "hot seat" in each group. Students can perform particularly successful responses for the entire class.

SAMPLE

The following are questions addressed to Black Elk in "Wasichus in the Hills":

- *Do you think you could live with the Wasichus? How might the Lakota and Wasichus work out their problems?*

- *Are traditional celebrations fun for you? What is your favorite part of growing up?*

- *Do you think you will become a famous and powerful person because you have visions?*

- *What do you think is going to happen to the Lakota people and to all Indian people?*

- *Who are you more afraid of, the Crow or the Wasichus?*

- *Are there other lifestyles you might prefer?*

Black Elk might answer the third question this way: "Crazy Horse has great visions; he knows much of what will happen in the future. People love him, but are afraid of him too because he partly lives in the world of pure visions. I see things, like the swallows flying above me, and this was part of a vision. I hear voices too, like the voice telling me to go home when people had just found out that Wasichus were near. But I am mainly just a boy who loves to race ponies and play with my friends."

LESSON 9
LITERATURE JOURNAL OR ESSAY: THE TONE OF SOCIAL CRITICISM

Although all the selections in this section are critical of society, they differ significantly in tone. In this lesson students will explore whether they find a particular author's tone to be one of open anger, sarcasm, sadness, or humor.

1. Have students compare the tone of two or three of the works in this section. Ask them to examine how the author creates the tone of the work. Have students quote sections of the work that especially express the author's tone.

2. Ask students to share their personal responses to the various tones of the works. Are there some they prefer and others that offend or bother them? Do they share some of the author's attitudes? Ask students to explain their responses.

LESSON 10
JOURNAL, DISCUSSION, OR ESSAY: REVIEW THE SCHOOL'S SOCIAL STUDIES TEXTBOOKS

Divide the class into groups, each of which is responsible for studying a novel or personal memoir about a given time period in American history. Alternatively, you may have the entire class read the same novel and study a given period together.

Have students write in their journals about the social, economic, and political issues, trends, and events in their novels. Students should include as many references to dates and places as possible.

SUGGESTED READING FOR THE PERIOD OF SLAVERY, THE CIVIL WAR, AND RECONSTRUCTION (1850–1890)
Kindred, Octavia Butler
Beloved, Toni Morrison

Jubilee, Margaret Walker
*Dessa Rose, Sherley Anne Williams

SUGGESTED READING FOR THE PERIOD LEADING UP TO AND
INCLUDING WORLD WAR I (EARLY 1900s–1920s)
Cold Sassy Tree, Olive Ann Burns
*O, Pioneers! Willa Cather
Sister Carrie, Theodore Dreiser
*Tracks, Louise Erdrich
The Great Gatsby, F. Scott Fitzgerald
*Call It Sleep, Henry Roth

SUGGESTED READING FOR THE PERIOD OF THE 1930s–1940s
*Out of the Furnace, Thomas Bell
*Invisible Man, Ralph Ellison
*Jews Without Money, Michael Gold
*No-No Boy, John Okada
*Y No Se lo Trago la Tierra / And the Earth Did Not Devour Him, Tomas Rivera
Grapes of Wrath, John Steinbeck
*The Road to Memphis, Mildred Taylor
*Roll of Thunder, Hear My Cry, Mildred Taylor

SUGGESTED READING FOR THE PERIOD OF THE 1950s–1960s
*How the Garcia Girls Lost Their Accents, Julia Alvarez
*Heart of a Woman, Maya Angelou
*Lakota Woman, Mary Crow Dog
*Nigger! Dick Gregory
*The Autobiography of Malcolm X, as told to Alex Haley
*Betsey Brown, Ntozake Shange
*Pocho, José Antonio Villareal
*Macho! Victor Villasenor
Meridian, Alice Walker

Have students compare what they learned about a culture from their
school's social studies and history texts to what they learned about that
same culture from reading literature (including selections from this
anthology) and conducting their own research. In groups, ask students to
compare the issues and events they have listed in their journals with information from relevant chapters in their social studies and history texts.

Have students include in their comparisons responses to the following
questions:

- *Are the issues in your novel and selections from* Hear My Voice *covered adequately in your school's texts? Is there information left out of the text that you would have included? Explain.*

- *Do the texts contain important information not included in the other sources? Explain.*

- *Are there interesting differences in the treatments of the subject? Explain.*

- *What are your thoughts about this process of text review? What conclusions, if any, can you draw? If you see problems with the content of school texts, how should they be solved? Who should solve them? Explain your proposals.*

VARIATION: NONFICTION

SUGGESTED LONGER WORKS
Labor's Untold Story, Richard O. Boyer and Herbert M. Morais
Custer Died for Your Sins: An Indian Manifesto, Vine Deloria, Jr.
Hearts of Sorrow: Vietnamese-American Lives, James Freeman
The New Chinatown, Peter Kwong
*The Black Americans: A History in Their Own Words, Milton Meltzer
*The Hispanic Americans, Milton Meltzer
*The Jewish Americans: A History in Their Own Words, Milton Meltzer
The Brick People, Alejandro Morales
*Native-American Testimony: A Chronicle of Indian-White Relations from Prophecy to the Present, 1492–1992, edited by Peter Nabokov, foreword by Vine Deloria, Jr.
Hispanic Arizona, James Officer
Cheyenne Autumn, Mari Sandoz
*Stranger from a Different Shore, Ronald Takaki
*Years of Infamy: The Untold Story of America's Concentration Camps, Micki Weglyn
*People's History of the United States, Howard Zinn

Note: You may also use works of nonfiction suggested for Lesson 2, page 55.

Have students read some works of nonfiction written from the point of view of people of a particular culture, then compare the issues and events emphasized in these books to those emphasized by the relevant sections of the school's social studies texts. After they have read the works of nonfiction, ask students whether there are any changes they would make in the school's texts. Would they add, delete, or rewrite sections or chapters? Ask them to fully explain their answers.

Have representatives from the different groups present their responses to the entire class.

LESSON 11
LITERATURE JOURNAL: THE PERSUASIVE QUALITIES OF A WORK

SUGGESTED WORKS FROM *HEAR MY VOICE*
Wasichus in the Hills, page 205
The Lesson, page 216
Each Year Grain, page 252
Tony's Story, page 265
This Is the Land, page 272

SUGGESTED LONGER WORKS
Out of This Furnace, Thomas Bell
Donald Duk, Frank Chin
Invisible Man, Ralph Ellison
Annie on My Mind, Nancy Garden
Mean Spirit, Linda Hogan
Grapes of Wrath, John Steinbeck
The Adventures of Huckleberry Finn, Mark Twain
Meridian, Alice Walker
*Homebase, Shawn Wong
Black Boy, Richard Wright
*Eight Men, Richard Wright

Have students read one of the works listed above. Ask:

- *Does the work effectively express a point of view?*

- *Is the selection persuasive and authoritative or does it seem unconvincing or propagandistic?*

Considering these questions can help readers improve their own writing.

1. Discuss with students the ways in which authors sometimes try to convey opinions about the real world through the art of fiction. Explain to students that some works of literature are written for the beauty of the prose while others have an underlying purpose of conveying serious messages, and that most works artfully combine the two. As students read one of the works listed above, have them keep track of which aspects of society the author is trying to present. Ask students to write

in their literature journals the author's views in their own words at various points in the novel.

2. Have students list aspects of the work that help make the author's views about society plausible or convincing to them. Tell students that many factors can make a work convincing, such as what the main characters are like, the tone, the setting, and the plot. Some questions you may provide to students include:

- *Does the author create characters who are trustworthy so that readers will accept their points of view?*

- *Do the characters respond to their situations in a reasonable manner?*

- *Does the author's choice of details describing the setting make his or her point plausible?*

- *Is the work convincing or unconvincing? Explain.*

LESSON 12
LITERATURE JOURNAL OR DISCUSSION: A PSYCHIATRIST OR SOCIAL WORKER
RESPONDS TO A CHARACTER

SUGGESTED WORKS FROM *HEAR MY VOICE*
Who Said We All Have to Talk Alike, page 7
The Bending of a Twig, page 145
Wasichus in the Hills, page 205
They Say Them Child Brides Don't Last, page 257
Tony's Story, page 265
From *I Know Why the Caged Bird Sings,* page 286

SUGGESTED LONGER WORKS
Go Tell It on the Mountain, James Baldwin
More Than Meets the Eye, Jeanne Betancourt
Kindred, Octavia Butler
Tracks, Louise Erdrich
The Drowning of Stephan Jones, Bette Greene
Black Elk Speaks, as told to John G. Neihardt
Cheyenne Autumn, Mari Sandoz
Road to Memphis, Mildred D. Taylor
Roll of Thunder, Hear My Cry, Mildred D. Taylor

Huckleberry Finn, Mark Twain
Black Boy, Richard Wright

Ask students to pretend they are a psychiatrist, social worker, or good friend of one of the characters in this section and they will conduct a series of meetings with the character. Suggest that students choose characters to write about or discuss who exert a negative or destructive influence on others, for instance, the sheriff in "Tony's Story," or the "gun thugs" in "They Say Them Child Brides Don't Last." Ask them to make a list of questions they would ask to help the character understand himself or herself. Also ask them which traits they would emphasize to the character so that his or her life could be happier and more productive.

Characters to consider in longer works include: Richard Wright's employers, grandmother, or father in *Black Boy,* or Huck's father, the "king," the "duke," or any of the other slave traders in *Huckleberry Finn.* Note for students that many of the characters who fit this assignment are minor characters.

Ask students to explain why this person comes to see them in the first place. Ask:

- *Is the client feeling excessive guilt, anger, or numbness?*

- *Did someone else convince the client to see you?*

- *What do you hypothesize are the reasons for your client's problems and behavior?*

LESSON 13

POEM: IMAGES OF THE UNITED STATES
based on "I Hear America Singing" by Walt Whitman

When Walt Whitman wrote the poem "I Hear America Singing" in the late 1800s, he chose images of a United States that was productively working, and his tone fit these images. His view of the United States was positive, uplifting, and optimistic.

An individual's overview of the United States would likely vary depending on the era in which that person lives or lived. People of different cultural groups also might focus on different aspects of American life at a given time. Ask students what they as individuals, and perhaps as members of a particular cultural group, see the United States doing at the present time.

Using Whitman's poem as a model, have students write a poem choosing images of what they see and hear and experience today in the United States. They might focus on one major aspect of life as Whitman did with working, or they might want the poem to be more freeform.

Tell students to follow the form of "I Hear America Singing" as closely as they wish, using their own counterparts for Whitman's different occupations and activities. Is the United States they see and hear working, singing, crying, questioning, rapping, shouting, pleading, fighting, trying, changing?

Guide students to develop a clear tone in their poems by choosing precise images. Students may wish to be optimistic, pessimistic, worried, urgent, angry, disgusted, sad, bemused, amused and so on.

STUDENT SAMPLE

I SEE AMERICA DRINKING

I see America drinking, many people I see.
Steel workers drinking fast after a hard day's work.
Farmers drinking, trying to relieve the grey of winter.
Teachers drinking to soothe their fatigue.
I see advertisers glamorize drinking: "It's the way to make friends,
    have laughs."
I see students drinking because it's the thing to do, and parents
    drinking to scare away the blues.
Storekeepers also drinking to help them pass through the day,
    construction workers drinking, wasting their pay.
Drinking and drinking, I see it each day. I wonder why it has to be
    that way.
People, young and old drinking each day …. drinking until it's …
    gone.

—*Maria Cobian Estrada*

PERSONAL IDENTITY

W HO AM I?" "What values are important to me?" "What kind of life will I choose?" "How do I want to be remembered?" "What is my path in life?" "How can I be true to myself?" These are universal questions that people of all cultures ask in the lifelong process of forming their identities. In the lessons in this unit students will consider these questions from personal and literary points of view and will consequently explore literature from a personal perspective.

LESSON I

POEM IN TWO VOICES: ANCESTRAL ROOTS
based on "Ending Poem" by Rosario Morales and Aurora Levins Morales

Rosario Morales and Aurora Levins Morales, mother and daughter, wrote "Ending Poem" about who they are and their ancestors' contributions to their lives. The poets feel that their ancestors' ways of life are part of them, but each poet believes she is also a new and unique individual.

Have pairs of students read "Ending Poem" aloud, each partner taking one of the two voices. Then have students write a poem based on "Ending Poem." In addition to writing about their own experiences, have students write in their mother's, father's, or other older relative's voice about his or her experiences. They may also write the poem collaboratively with their relative. If students write the poems themselves, they may wish to interview a relatives to obtain the necessary information.

INSTRUCTIONS

Part 1—Provide biographical information about yourself and one of your parents or older relatives.

Begin your poem with the line "I am what I am." This is your line. Continue to write lines alternatively in your voice and in the voice of your relative. In your voice, tell about your background; in your relative's voice, tell about his or her background. The facts you choose to write about may include: place of origin, socioeconomic background, languages spoken and heard as a child, and basic values. Provide details that demonstrate these facts.

Part 2—Find traits you and your ancestors share.

Continue this part of the poem in one or both voices. Go back as many generations as you wish: hundreds of years or one or two generations. Specify the continent, country, city, or state your ancestors were from, and describe aspects of your ancestor's lives that are part of you, but are not all of you. If you can, describe traits you have internalized from two or three different generations of your family.

TWO SAMPLE VERSES FOR PART 2 OF THIS POEM

Russia is in me. (Asia too?)
The towns, the cities, the jammed streets, the domed synagogues.
But I am not Russia.

I am not New York City.
The color, the variety, my family, those are in me,
but they are not all of me.

You may already know about features of your distant ancestors' places of origin and ways of life that are part of you. If you do not, ask your parents and older relatives. Another important source of information is the library. Look up information about the areas in which your ancestors lived, and find characteristics of those places that resonate in you.

Part 3—Ending section

You may begin this section with "I am new." or "I move on." Describe how you are entering new territory or how you are different from your ancestors.

READING YOUR POEM

Practice reading your poem with your relative or with another person taking your relative's part, and at a class party read your poem with the other person.

LESSON 2
LITERATURE JOURNAL/COLLAGE: THE DEVELOPMENT OF
A CHARACTER'S IDENTITY

SUGGESTED LONGER WORKS
Bless Me Ultima, Rudolfo Anaya
I Know Why the Caged Bird Sings, Maya Angelou
Go Tell It on the Mountain, James Baldwin

When The Legends Die, Hal Borland
*The Last of the Menu Girls, Denise Chávez
*Donald Duk, Frank Chin
*The House on Mango Street, Sandra Cisneros
Crime and Punishment, Fyodor Dostoyevski
*Invisible Man, Ralph Ellison
The Diary of Anne Frank, Anne Frank
The Miracle Worker, William Gibson
*The Autobiography of Malcolm X, as told to Alex Haley
A Doll's House, Henrick Ibsen
*China Boy, Gus Lee
*Riversong, Craig Leslie
*Winterkill, Craig Leslie
*Beloved, Toni Morrison
*Nilda, Nicholasa Mohr
*Jasmine, Bharati Mukherjee
*All I Asking for Is My Body, Milton Murayama
*George Washington Gomez, Americo Paredes
*Foreigner, Nahid Rachlin
*Always Running, Louis J. Rodriguez
*Hunger of Memory, Richard Rodriguez
Catcher in the Rye, J. D. Salinger
Hamlet, William Shakespeare
Pygmalion, George Bernard Shaw
*Ceremony, Leslie Silko
The Red Pony, John Steinbeck
The Color Purple, Alice Walker
*Sea Glass, Laurence Yep

Characters may change significantly over the course of many of the works in this section because they take the opportunity to adapt in response to a situation. One good way to gain a perspective of such change within a work is to represent the stages of the character's life pictorially. This project applies better to longer works than to short stories.

LITERATURE JOURNAL

1. Ask students to identify several important stages of the main character's life in the work they are studying. What are the important events in each stage?

Explain to the class there is room for interpretation regarding the boundaries of stages (or periods) in a character's life. The edges may be blurry. Have students share their responses to Question 1 so they can learn from each other. There need not be total consensus as long as responses are reasonable.

2. Have students create or find pictures in magazines that represent the qualities of the character at these different stages. Guide them to choose images that visually represent the character's predominant values, priorities, and feelings. The pictures can be literal or metaphorical.

3. Have students mount the images on paper, and as a class or in groups make educated guesses about the meanings of other students' pictures.

LESSON 3
ESSAY: THE TRANSFORMATION OF A CHARACTER IN A MAJOR WORK

SUGGESTED LONGER WORKS
*Bless Me Ultima, Rudolfo Anaya
*I Know Why the Caged Bird Sings, Maya Angelou
*Go Tell It on the Mountain, James Baldwin
When The Legends Die, Hal Borland
*The Last of the Menu Girls, Denise Chávez
*Donald Duk, Frank Chin
*The House on Mango Street, Sandra Cisneros
Crime and Punishment, Fyodor Dostoyevski
*Invisible Man, Ralph Ellison
The Diary of Anne Frank, Anne Frank
The Miracle Worker, William Gibson
*The Autobiography of Malcolm X, as told to Alex Haley
A Doll's House, Henrick Ibsen
*China Boy, Gus Lee
*Riversong, Craig Leslie
*Winterkill, Craig Leslie
*Beloved, Toni Morrison
*Nilda, Nicholasa Mohr
*Jasmine, Bharati Mukherjee
*All I Asking for Is My Body, Milton Murayama

George Washington Gomez, Americo Paredes
Foreigner, Nahid Rachlin
Always Running, Louis J. Rodriguez
Hunger of Memory, Richard Rodriguez
Catcher in the Rye, J. D. Salinger
Hamlet, William Shakespeare
Pygmalion, George Bernard Shaw
Ceremony, Leslie Silko
The Red Pony, John Steinbeck
The Color Purple, Alice Walker
Sea Glass, Laurence Yep

PREWRITING

Lesson 2, page 76, provides an excellent prewriting activity for this lesson. Students can do the entire activity or just the writing activity described in Section I.

WRITING THE DRAFT

Ask students to explain what the main character learns during the course of the novel or play and to provide details and quotes to justify their points. Have students speculate about why the character changes and what in his or her life prompts or causes the transformations? Ask students to predict, as best they can, what the main character will be like after the time frame of the work.

LESSON 4
ESSAY: THE TRANSFORMATION OF CHARACTERS IN SHORTER WORKS

SUGGESTED WORKS FROM *HEAR MY VOICE*
Paths Upon Water, page 12
From *I Know Why the Caged Bird Sings*, page 286
Flying Home, page 298
Autumn Gardening, page 317
South Brooklyn, 1947, page 325

Have students write an essay describing how the main character or characters of the work change in the course of the story. Instruct them to support their analysis of what the character learns with details and quotes from the work. Ask them to identify how the learning takes place, and again, to support their analyses with detail and quotes. Have students explain what they find significant about the character's newfound knowledge.

LESSON 5
AUTOBIOGRAPHICAL FRAGMENT: ESSAY ON A PERSONAL TRANSFORMATION

This project can serve as an introduction or conclusion to a study of literature focusing on a major transformation in a character.

PREWRITING

1. Ask students to list chronologically events or episodes in their lives, such as learning to ride a bike, crossing streets on their own, their eleventh birthday, a first date, or involvement in an accident.

     Have students share with the class some of the items on their lists.

2. Now have students graph the events and episodes they have generated. Instruct them to place the events and episodes of their lives in chronological order on the "x" axis of a graph, and on the "y" axis to represent how much they learned about themselves and the world; the larger the "y" value, the more knowledge gained in the experience. Then have students rate each of the important events according to how much they learned about themselves and the world. Ask students to choose an event or episode that has a dramatic "y" value on their graph. It is likely they can write much about it.

WRITING THE DRAFT

Direct students to describe exactly what happened in the event. They should explain what they learned by describing what they were like before and after this turning point. Then ask students to predict how this event might shape their future.

LESSON 6
LITERATURE JOURNAL: IDENTITY AND CULTURAL TRADITIONS

SUGGESTED WORKS FROM *HEAR MY VOICE*
Paths Upon Water, page 12
Different Cultural Levels Eat Here, page 28
Sonrisas, page 62
A Song in the Front Yard, page 64
Doors, page 65

The purpose of these journal entries is to explore the extent to which one's cultural heritage (history, traditions, values, and attitudes) is part of who one is. The link between personal identity and culture varies between individuals, cultures, and historical periods.

As students read the novels, plays, stories, and poems in this section, ask them to respond to the following questions as they find them applicable:

- *Can people separate themselves from their culture? Can benefits be gained by attempting to do so? Provide specific examples from literary selections.*

- *To what degree are social pressures involved when people separate themselves from their culture? To what degree are force and violence involved? Provide specific examples and quotes from the selections.*

- *What are the benefits of fostering one's own culture? Why do people feel drawn to their own culture? Provide specific examples and quotes from the literature in this anthology to support your response.*

- *Do people sometimes feel ambivalent about their culture?*

LESSON 7

PERSONAL JOURNAL OR PANEL: IDENTITY AND CULTURAL TRADITIONS

See the discussion/debate on the value of traditions in Family and Generations, Lesson 17, page 51.

Ask students to respond to the following questions as they find them applicable:

- *What is culture? List as much as you can about the history, traditions, values, language, and dialect of your family and community. Review the list. Is everything on the list a part of your culture? If not, why not?*

- *Do you feel that you know much or little about your culture? Are there aspects you would like to know more about? Explain.*

- *To what degree do you accept and enjoy your heritage and consciously make it part of your daily life? For instance, do you tell your classmates or your teachers stories about your culture?*

- *To what extent do you wish to be identified with your original heritage? Does identification with a particular heritage become an asset or a burden? Explain.*

- *Are you taught about your culture in school? Give examples of what you learn about your culture in school and describe your feelings about these examples.*

- *Are some cultures taught in your school more thoroughly than others? If so, why do you think this happens? Do you have any suggestions of what your school or class could study in order to more fully explore your own or another's culture?*

- *Are there other ways school administration or faculty could help include cultures that may be excluded? Explain.*

Note: Following clear ground rules that prohibit derogatory remarks, a panel of students could use the above prompts to speak to the entire class or school on the above issues. When a group of about twenty predominantly Mexican-American students spoke about these issues to a primarily European-American faculty in Southern California, the discussion was enlightening. Many of the students felt they were "seen" for the first time. They reported having said things in the forum they had never even said to each other.

LESSON 10
A PICTURE AS A PERSONAL METAPHOR

Virginia Cotsis of Ventura, California, showed me this exciting and thought-provoking project. The activity fosters self-awareness and pride and serves as an introduction or conclusion to one of the literary works that address personal identity. This is also a good lesson in metaphor.

Students choose a pictorial metaphor for themselves, interpret each other's pictures, and then write a personal essay on the process. I always participate along with the students. Although the project seems complicated at first, the individual steps are easy to accomplish and yield great success.

FINDING THE PICTORIAL METAPHOR

Have each student choose a single magazine photo that represents him or her metaphorically. Direct students to choose an inanimate object, landscape, or animal rather than a person.

Before searching for these pictorial metaphors, have students practice interpreting photographs. For instance, display a picture of a camera and encourage interpretations such as, "The person is a careful observer," or "The person is complex." Help students to understand the difference between these metaphorical interpretations and literal interpretations such as, "The person enjoys taking pictures."

Instruct students to think about what qualities of themselves they would most like to portray. Remind them to use the photograph metaphorically and to avoid superficial messages like, "I enjoy taking pictures." Ask students to choose their photographs at home or somewhere else private so that other students will not be able to identify their photographs. When students bring their photographs to class, keep secret the names of the owners, and identify photographs on the back using a long number like a birthday or social security number.

CLASS INTERPRETATION OF PICTURES

Assure students that many metaphorical interpretations might arise from one picture and that they might gain insight into their own personalities from new interpretations of their photographs.

This is a high-energy activity, and the teacher must keep students moving at a rapid pace so that all photos can be interpreted in one class period. You may wish to explain the following process to the class the day before you do interpretations, so you will have the full period for the activity itself.

At this point, you should have all the photos. The students should be seated in groups of four or five. Each student will need a packet of small note paper.

Distribute one photo to each student, and then give the signal to begin. In one minute, have each student write the following on one slip of paper:
- the I.D. number of the photo, which is written on the back
- his or her metaphorical interpretation of the photo
- his or her signature

At the end of the minute, have each student pass the photograph to the next person in the group and repeat the process using a new slip of paper. When all photographs have been interpreted within the group, ask students to pass their packets of photos to the next group, and continue the process until each student has interpreted each photograph.

You may wish to remind students they should not make negative or destructive comments about their classmates' pictures.

You may want to enlist help in sorting the slips of paper into piles by identification number. The following day, amidst much anticipation, each student receives the packet of slips about his or her picture and reads the various interpretations of the photograph. Students' comments about the photographs are often positive and insightful, and they stimulate constructive thinking about personal identity.

PERSONAL ESSAY ABOUT THE PHOTO

1. Have students describe their photos and explain what they originally intended the picture to express. Ask them to provide details about their lives that support their choices of metaphor.

2. Have students discuss other students' interpretations of their photographs. Ask students to write about which interpretations are similar to what they intended, which new interpretations they feel are apt, and which ones they feel do not fit. Again, ask students to provide details from their lives to support their responses.

3. Ask students to evaluate the entire project from beginning to end.

- *What did you learn?*

- *How could the process be improved?*

- *Do you feel you got as much as you could out of the activity?*

This essay provides a useful vehicle for capturing and deepening students' thoughts about their identities. Jaime, one of my ninth grade students, for example, learned valuable information about himself that could have an important effect on his life. He, like many of his friends, is not academically oriented, and is often "in trouble" in school. Jaime loves trucks and cars and constantly draws them, and I suspected that he would use a picture of a car for his metaphor. So he did; the picture was of a shiny truck under a palm tree. A student named Adam's interpretation of this photo made a particularly strong impression on Jaime. As Jaime said in his essay: "Another quality that Adam said I had, that I didn't originally think about myself was that I would live the tropical, luxurious lifestyle of an interesting person. I never even thought about all that. I was always thinking about being a cool guy and that I would be bad and act bad. But I decided to make a goal that I would not be in the streets or act hot...."

This would be a good project to do in the beginning and at the end of a year, or at the start and at the completion of high school, to help students measure the progress they have made.

✳ ✳ ✳ ✳ ✳ ✳ ✳ ✳ ✳ ✳ ✳ ✳ ✳ ✳ ✳

CELEBRATIONS

*I*N A MULTICULTURAL SOCIETY at its best, people would not just tolerate differences; they would appreciate and share the strengths of their diversity. The selections and projects in this section encourage celebration of the positive features of our own and each other's cultures.

LESSON 1

CELEBRATORY POEM
based on "Call Letters: Mrs. V. B." by Maya Angelou

Maya Angelou's upbeat expression of self-esteem provides a good model of a celebratory poem. Identification with her African-American heritage has given her a pool of strength from which to draw, and her celebration of herself as an individual honors her culture.

Ask students to write a poem that celebrates their own life. First, have them think of four topics, one for each stanza, that relate to their lives. Then, suggest that they play around with two rhyming lines until the stanza sounds right to them.

SAMPLES

Mountains, sure I'll climb them.
If they've got the views
To paint over the blues
I'll climb them.

Music? I love to dance.
If it's got the sound
To move me around
I'll boogie.

Books, yeah I'll write them.
I'll express my ideas
Overcome my fears
See, my name in print!

I'll play it.
If I can't get through the line
I'll run around from behind
And then we'll win it.

You may wish to have each student write two verses, and then construct a class poem. It would be a nice way to open or close a semester, and the poem could be prominently displayed.

LESSON 2
POEM: CHANGING CONNOTATIONS OF THE WORD "BLACK"
based on "Ain't That Bad" by Maya Angelou

In this lesson and the following five lessons students will use their own experience, personal observations, and ideas from reading to write poems in a variety of forms. You may have students use standard forms including cinquains, acrostics, haikus, or sonnets, or you may encourage them to write poems more closely based on particular models in the anthology. Finally, you may give students the option to write a freeform poem. As students work on the assignments, suggest they consult with family members and classmates for more ideas. If you wish, assign students to use words and phrases from languages other than English as well as various dialects to accent this celebration of different cultural groups.

The English language has developed to make "black," "brown," and "dark" concepts with negative connotations, while "white" and "light" often portray something positive. Ask students to think of sayings and phrases that show this. Discuss how these connotations can affect the self-esteem of people of color.

Author Langston Hughes was a pioneer in counteracting negative associations of blackness. In his poem "Dream Variation," Hughes associated the color black with the restful, cool, gentle, tender night.

Have students write a poem in which they associate black, brown, or other dark shades with beauty, like warm rich cocoa, hot coffee or tea, shiny black satin, golden brown chestnuts, or deep navy blue velvet sky. Tell them that their poems may describe an object or tell a story that involves a beautiful dark object or person.

Urge students to go beyond literal descriptions and to use metaphors and similes. Point out how Maya Angelou does this when she writes about blackness:

"Black like the hour of night
When your love turns and wriggles close to your side
Black as the earth which has given birth
To nations, and when all else is gone will abide."

LESSON 3

POEM: THE PRIDE OF A GREAT BALLPLAYER
based on "To Satch: American Gothic" by Samuel Allen (Paul Vesey)

Satchel Paige, one of the greatest baseball pitchers the world has ever known, reached the major leagues only very late in his career. This celebration by Paul Vesey carries particular force because it was racism that kept Paige in the minor leagues.

Have students write a tribute to a talented sports figure who does not receive deserved recognition because of nationality, ethnicity, religion, gender, or another unfair reason. The poem may be set in the past or the present about someone in professional, amateur, or school sports. If students can't think of anyone, sugggest they create a fictional character.

Encourage students to demonstrate the superb athletic talents of the person by describing in detail a fantastic play, possibly using exaggeration.

- *How fast does this person run?*

- *How graceful is he?*

- *How high can she jump?*

- *How much control does he have of his body?*

- *What kind of teammate is she?*

LESSON 4

POEM: THE PRIDE OF A GREAT DANCER

based on "The Latest Latin Dance Craze" by Victor Hernández Cruz

This poem shows tremendous appreciation for Latin dance by presenting an image of a strong, agile man giving a new meaning to the word "dance."

Have students write a poem honoring some kind of dancing or the music that accompanies it. For emphasis, they may wish to exaggerate special or unique aspects of the dance and music. Provide a few examples:

- *If you write about southern Appalachian square or contra dancing developed by people of Scots-Irish heritage, you may wish to focus on the complexity and speed of the steps.*

- *If you write about slow soul and jazz music, you may decide to emphasize the relaxing quality of the music, and the grace it inspires in dancers.*

- *Hard rock and heavy metal may suggest an emphasis on excitement, loudness, and intensity.*

SAMPLE

Cool Jazz
Coltrane melody begins half way into his
walk across the dance floor to me.
Eyes locked to mine, he
moves like golden honey that is almost frozen.
So slow and gorgeous.
Hmm ... This is all part of the dance.
When the notes begin to curl out,
there is just the slightest taste of invitation to the dance in
his hips, but
you really need several instant replays to see this.

LESSON 5

POEM: REFLECTION ON A FOOD

based on "Rice Planting" by Amy Uyematsu

After reading "Rice Planting" by Amy Uyematsu, have students write their own poems about a food. Students may want to write about a food that is important to their own or someone's else's culture or family, or they may wish to make up an example. Help students to notice the detail with which Uyematsu writes about rice, and encourage them to model their poems on hers.

PREWRITING PROMPTS

- *Describe the methods your family or you use to prepare this dish, possibly contrasting your methods of preparation with those of other people.*

- *What are other things one eats with this dish?*

- *In what situations is this food eaten? Include special occasions like parties and holidays.*

- *Does the food have curative powers?*

- *Can you order it at a restaurant? If so, is the restaurant version as good as the home-made variety?*

- *What are your feelings about this dish? How do others feel about it?*

- *Is it a special occasion or an everyday kind of food?*

In order to generate ideas for this poem, suggest students use their experience, consult with others, and use reference books, including, of course, cookbooks.

After the poems are drafted and edited, students may wish to have a food and poetry party in which people bring in food they prepare at home or in home economics classes.

LESSON 6

POEM: CHILDHOOD ACTIVITY WITH AN ADULT
based on "Ravioli" by Anna Bart

An adult fondly remembers preparing ravioli with her grandmother in the poem "Ravioli." Children often love to help adults work and play, whether it be in the kitchen, in the garden, in the garage, or on the basketball court. Working with and learning from adults is a source of inspiration and education for many of us.

Have students write a poem in which they tell the story of making, doing, or fixing something with an older family member or friend when they were a child. Tell them to provide details about the adult, the setting of this activity, and the process. Instruct students to develop the tone and atmosphere of the poem through their choice of details.

- *Describe the process of the activity. It could be a variety of activities from preparing tamales to playing basketball.*

- *What do you remember of the overall appearance and atmosphere of the setting of this activity?*

- *Describe your relative or friend. Describe the equipment you used.*

- *What was your role in the production?*

- *What were and are your feelings toward the people and the process you were involved in? Do you remember the activity fondly? Do you feel a strong nostalgia for that period in your life? Is there some ambivalence? Were there some negative features of those times?*

LESSON 7

POEM: TRADITIONAL FAMILY CELEBRATIONS
based on "Powwow 79, Durango" by Paula Gunn Allen

Traditional gatherings are important in most cultures. Many Native Americans look forward to powwows. Ask students to discuss "Powwow 79, Durango."

- *What are the daughter's feelings about powwows? How do they change during the course of the poem?*

- *What are the mother's feelings about her culture as it is expressed in the powwow? How does the poet convey these feelings?*

Have students write their own poems in which they describe a traditional celebration in their family. In addition to describing the celebrations, encourage students to analyze their feelings about the event and incorporate their feelings into the poem. Present the following questions about the tradition for students to consider as they write their poems:

- *What is its purpose?*

- *What exactly happens at this gathering?*

- *Who is typically present?*

- *Is the atmosphere calm, spiritual, noisy, or rowdy?*

- *How do people dress?*

- *What kinds of food do people eat?*

- *Are "outsiders" present?*

- *How do the different generations relate?*

- *What is positive about this gathering for you?*

- *Is there anything troublesome or negative about this gathering for you?*

LESSON 8
I-SEARCH PAPER ON CULTURAL LEADERS

There exist many individuals and groups who help raise the consciousness of their people. They encourage members of their cultural group to define themselves by their cultural strengths, rather than by their often invisible or negative status in the popular media.

Some examples of such people and groups are Spike Lee, Malcolm X, Stokeley Carmichael, Frederick Douglass, Jesse Jackson, the Black Panthers, Black Consciousness Movement, Student Non-violent Coordinating Committee, Vernon Bellacourt, John Trudell, Dennis Banks, Russell Means, American Indian Movement, Cesar Chavez, Dolores Huerta, Louis Valdez, Teatro Campesino, and United Farmworkers Union.

This is just a short list of people, groups, and movements that students can study. Encourage them to consult with other classmates, teachers, librarians, and periodicals and reference books to expand their lists. Have them choose one of these individuals or groups as the subject of their I-search paper.

I learned about the following format for an I-search report from Mark Oldani, of Portland, Oregon.

DESCRIPTION OF THE I-SEARCH PAPER

Tell students that the I-Search paper on a cultural leader or movement should tell the story of their research on the topic. Explain that in the paper they will describe their thinking process, rather than simply presenting the results of their search. Suggest that students think of themselves as creative scientists making and testing hypotheses, rather than as scribes who copy the views of others. Their questions, guesses, previous beliefs, and knowledge will guide the research as they base their I-search papers on their I-search journals.

THE I-SEARCH JOURNAL

Students should keep a daily search journal that has two parts:

Part A: a record of questions, thoughts, and feelings while reading and interviewing

Part B: a summary of the views of other people with bibliographical references and important quotes. This record of the views of others is what students usually consider a research paper to be. Summarizing the views of others is just part of doing an I-search paper.

Suggest to students that the best way to keep this daily journal is to divide their pages into two columns labeled Part A and Part B.

THE FORM OF THE I-SEARCH PAPER

The final I-search paper has three sections: Introduction, Body, and Opinion

a. Introduction

In this section, students should describe for the reader their prior knowledge, beliefs, assumptions, and preconceptions about the topic. Students should include all their initial questions and explain what attracted them to the topic in the first place. For example, one student may have chosen to study the Black Panthers because their name sounded intriguing. Questions the student may ask include: *How did they get their name? What kinds of activities did they do? Were they involved in a war? Are they like a gang or are they against gangs?* Perhaps they already know that they were an African-American group, and they wonder if the Black Panthers agreed with Martin Luther King, Jr.'s views. Other questions they might have are: *When exactly did they form as a group?* and *Do they still exist? If they no longer exist, what happened to them?*

b. Body of the Search

Have students present the narrative of their search. They should include the main points they have discovered and should explain their thought processes as they conducted their research.

c. Opinion of the Search

   Once students have completed their research, ask them to consider their opinions about the importance of the topic.

- *Who could benefit from the results of your research?*

- *How could your research be used?*

- *Could it be used in schools? How? Why? Why not? At what grade levels?*

- *Should there be a television documentary on your topic?*

- *Could a dramatic work for the movies or television be produced using the results of your research? If so, what might be the broader subject matter?*

LESSON 9
ESSAY OR LITERATURE JOURNAL WITH VISUAL DISPLAY: STRENGTHS OF A CULTURE

In the literature in this section of the anthology, positive qualities of people of different cultures are emphasized.

1. Ask students to describe the positive traits of characters who are presented in works they are reading and then to quote passages that express or demonstrate these traits. Perhaps the style of writing, as well as the content of the story or poem, celebrates the character as well as his or her family or culture.

2. In groups or as a class, have students create a visual display of magazine photos and drawings that depict the positive qualities expressed about characters of a variety of cultures in works they are studying. For instance, pictures depicting a calm spiritual place that is at the same time inviting and homey might describe the woman who makes swell doughnuts (*Hear My Voice*, page 367).

LESSON 10
TRIBUTE PARTY: A FAREWELL PROJECT

The object of this lesson is to show how people coming from diverse backgrounds, whose perceptions of each other are obscured and distorted by stereotypes from the popular media, can come to a respectful understanding of each other's cultures.

...dents to imagine that the characters from the literature in this ... are invited to a huge party. At this gala affair, characters make ...ts of tribute that show respect and appreciation for each other's ...es.

After choosing four or five characters from any of the works in this anthology or the related readings who will "speak" at this party, have students write in their journals what they might say to show respectful appreciation of another character's culture or heritage. The person making a tribute may comment on one or more of the following:

- *new understanding of the struggles the other character and others of his or her culture have had to face*

- *commonalities among people of different cultures*

- *how stereotypes were shattered*

- *what a character of a different culture says or does that is likable*

- *what can be learned about life from the other character's culture*

Here are some samples of tributes that might be made at this party:

Sylvia from "The Lesson" might toast characters from the Joad family in The Grapes Of Wrath *or the woman in "They Say Them Child Brides Don't Last" by saying, "I always thought white folks were rich and kind of ignorant. Imagine buying a toy for your baby that costs more than $1000 when its going to get broken anyway. The Joads were different and they opened up my eyes. They suffered just like us, and tried hard to make a better life. For all their hard farming, they didn't have anything to show for it, and on top of it, people looked down on them like they were trash.*

The main character in Bless Me, Ultima *may well say to Set in "She Is Beautiful in Her Whole Being": "Our Chicano way of life is so much like yours. Just like you guys, we see a spiritual connection between people today and our ancestors, and between people and nature.....*"

WRITE A SCENE FOR A RADIO PLAY

As an alternative or addition to the class display, have groups, pairs, or individuals write a scene of a radio play. Ask them to develop a setting, a host or hostess, and occasion for the party, and to create a dialogue between the characters.